On Foreign Soil

On Foreign Soil

Government Programs in U.S.-Mexico Relations

Beth Sims *with* **Tom Barry**

No. 2 in The U.S.-Mexico Series

Resource Center Press
Albuquerque, New Mexico

Acknowledgments

In writing this book, we benefited from the direct contributions of many friends and colleagues whose footwork, insights, commentary, and analysis were instrumental to the final product. The staff at the Resource Center formed the foundation that allowed the book to take place. Especially important were the research assistance by Erik Leaver and Steve Whitman; the feedback and editorial suggestions given by Harry Browne and Hannah Walraven; the administrative support offered by executive director Debra Preusch; and the publications skills of production manager John Hawley. Vital in detecting errors, correcting misconceptions, and offering important insights were the following experts who commented on parts of the manuscript and shared their information: David Brooks, Roderic Camp, Jorge Castañeda, Richard Craig, Peter Lupsha, Andrew Reding, Fred Schellenberg, and Steve Wager. We also gratefully acknowledge the financial support of the John D. and Catherine T. MacArthur Foundation, whose generous support made the work possible.

Contents

Conflict
and Cooperation

Times have changed. As recently as 1989 a leading expert on U.S.-Mexico relations observed that "it is not so much that the two countries do not understand each other—and this is particularly true at the governmental level—but rather that they disagree fundamentally in a number of areas."[1] As of the early 1990s, however, the two governments not only appear to understand each other quite well but have increasingly seen eye to eye on issues ranging from economics to international affairs. They have signed a free trade agreement, set up binational working groups to study shared problems and to recommend solutions, and accelerated joint responses to such concerns as drug trafficking and environmental degradation. Great asymmetries in power and wealth still overshadow the relationship, of course, giving greater weight to U.S. wishes and policy demands, and the needs of those people who make up the grassroots are not at the forefront of policy concerns in either country. But official relations since the late 1980s have been more harmonious than at any time since before the Mexican Revolution, with the brief exception of genial relations during the presidency of Miguel Alemán (1946-1952).[2]

The increasingly cordial tone of U.S.-Mexico relations during the 1980s reflected the rise to power of like-minded neoliberal forces in each country.[3] Carlos Salinas de Gortari and George Bush had an especially warm relationship. Both men were dedicated to deregulation, privatization, government cutbacks, the promotion of large corporate interests, global economic integration, and the free market. Both men gave global economic issues a higher priority than other items on the sociopolitical agenda, such as democratization or environmental protection. Under the two presidents, economic ties proliferated between the two countries, nationalist tensions subsided, and analysts began speaking of a new era of cooperation and converging interests.

The election of Bill Clinton to the U.S. presidency in 1992 was expected to reduce U.S.-Mexico consensus on some issues, especially worker protections, democratization, and the environment. Analysts predicted that Clinton, who was elected by U.S. voters concerned about domestic economic problems, environmental degradation, and human rights, would emphasize these issues more than his predecessors. Given Clinton's constituency, neglecting these concerns could backfire if he intended to run for re-election in 1996.

The long-term threat to Clinton's re-election may well be correct, but as of mid-1993, Clinton's policies toward Mexico have closely adhered to those laid out under Bush. In fact, the amount of continuity between the Bush and Clinton administrations' Mexico policies is "amazing," according to the Department of State's desk officer for Mexico, and there have been "no significant changes in the way things are done."[4] For example, Clinton, an advocate of market approaches, trade and investment liberalization, and U.S. economic expansion, has supported the North American Free Trade Agreement (NAFTA) as negotiated by the Bush and Salinas governments.[5]

Clinton endorsed NAFTA with the stipulation that the three NAFTA partners also negotiate side agreements to work out protections for the environment and labor, and to offset potential job loss due to import surges. The negotiations on the parallel accords have just been concluded as of this writing, but—at least from the point of view of NAFTA critics—they still fall short in terms of enforceability and the scope of protections.[6] Although they represent some improvement to NAFTA as negotiated by the Bush administration, the new accords do not indicate that Clinton will make issues like labor rights an overriding priority in relations with Mexico. Rather, like Bush and Reagan, Clinton will continue the course toward an economically integrated North America—the same goal sought by Mexico's political and economic leaders. Shared markets and shared production are the twin lights seen at the end of a tunnel of economic uncertainty and crisis, for both the United States and Mexico. Although Clinton is likely to be forced by domestic economic needs to cut back on aid programs to Mexico, the emphasis on expanding economic and political relations between the two countries will almost surely remain secure under the Democratic administration.

Official programs carried out by both governments are helping advance the integration that is under way. Although official relations are only one part of a broader socioeconomic process of integration, they are worth highlighting because they shape the framework within which most other interactions—trade and investment, for example—take place.[7] Most of this book focuses on U.S. government programs and the agencies that sponsor them, not because the United States is more worthy of study but because the United States has greater resources and therefore far more programs targeting Mexico than vice versa (see Chart). In addition, as the dominant partner, Washington is helping to shape the ongoing integration in favor of the United States, while making sure that Mexico's ruling party, the Institutional Revolutionary Party (PRI), stays powerful enough to carry out desired changes in the Mexican economy.

Looking closely at the U.S. side is also important because the deal worked out with Mexico is intended to have an impact regionally and globally. It is a significant component of Washington's strategy for coalescing a hemisphere-wide economic bloc dominated by the market, business entities, and financial structures of the United States. Washington also hopes to use NAFTA and other features of the U.S.-Mexico integration to influence negotiations on the rules for international trade and investment.

Converging Policies, Persistent Tensions

The United States and Mexico have had a troubled and uncertain relationship. Years of conflict have alternated with years of cooperation and still other periods of neglect and indifference. But the two countries are forever bound together by proximity and interdependence, if divided by asymmetry, culture, and language. "We have with Mexico a marriage without possibility of divorce," U.S. Ambassador John Gavin observed, catching in one comment the simultaneous ambivalence and necessity of the relationship.[8]

It has been the necessity of the relationship that has drawn the most official attention since the 1980s. Political and economic realities—economic woes at home, the end of the Cold War, international economic integration, and a global recession—forced each government to rethink the terms and objectives of the relationship. It is drawing Gavin's analogy too far to say the U.S. and

Mexican governments "renewed their vows," but that they committed themselves to deepening and improving official ties is clear.

The binational relationship is now treated as a potential source of prosperity and growth by both governments. It is also seen as a vehicle for resolving long-term problems like drug trafficking and undocumented migration that have as often caused contention as collaboration. Both government programs and nongovernmental linkages have proliferated over the last decade, responding not only to their own logic but also to government-sponsored stimulation.

Chart. *U.S. Executive Branch Departments and Agencies with Programs in Mexico*

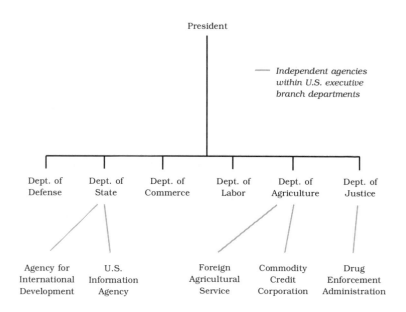

Independent agencies within U.S. executive branch departments

Independent Establishments and Government Corporations

- Environmental Protection Agency
- Export-Import Bank
- Inter-American Foundation
- National Endowment for Democracy

But focusing too closely—as some do—on the converging interests, even converging destinies, of the United States and Mexico is misleading.[9] North-South tensions still strain the relationship and pull important long-term national interests of the two countries in different directions. Mexico's need for jobs and investment, for instance, makes its view of U.S. runaway plants much more positive than the view taken by U.S. workers or congressional representatives. Likewise the two countries find themselves on opposite sides as far as undocumented Mexican migration to the United States is concerned.

International politics is not necessarily a zero sum game in which one wins and the other must lose. But asymmetries of wealth, power, and size do translate into policy effects that are the source of greater wins for the United States, more frequent losses for Mexico. "The United States is bigger, stronger, and richer than Mexico," wrote the Bilateral Commission on the Future of United States-Mexican Relations. "Under these conditions bargaining tends to be unequal."[10] The United States is dominant in more than just bilateral terms. The country is also a key player in global markets, international lending institutions, trade-negotiating forums like the General Agreement on Tariffs and Trade (GATT), and other international arenas important to Mexico's economic success.[11]

Washington's stamp of approval for the Mexican government, its economic aid, trade, loan support, and debt assistance all have come with strings attached. These have been used to encourage and enforce Mexican economic policies that open the door for increased U.S. trade and investment and slash the role of government in the economy. In addition, the Mexican government has had to go along with other U.S. initiatives when its own interests might well have led to different policy choices. It has had to pull out the stops in the war on drugs, for example, not only because of its own interest in eliminating challenges from traffickers but also to win White House certification and congressional approval, which are in turn conditions for aid, trade, and lending packages.

But recent Mexican governments have not been just punching bags for Washington. The collapse of aging economic strategies, conditions attached to international debt and aid packages, political repercussions from the government's inadequate response to the 1985 earthquake, and upheavals like the 1988 elections shook up Mexican political structures. These events boosted the fortunes of Mexican policy makers who shared the economic worldview of counterparts in Washington and who believed strongly that solving Mexico's problems would require close alliances with highly developed countries like the United States. Since the days when Salinas first took over as budget and planning minister under President Miguel de la Madrid, Mexican political leaders have often found themselves on common ground with Washington. The new cooperation that analysts observe is actually a partnership between sectors of the U.S. and Mexican economic and political elite that share the same diagnosis of Mexican and global economic problems and the same prescriptions for overcoming them.

Aims and Interests

The stakes are high for both the United States and Mexico as they work out a new relationship in the rapidly changing global economy. Priorities like making sure that Mexico remains stable politically and that both countries are economically healthy occupy the top of the agenda. Most bilateral efforts, as well as unilateral government programs, are designed to serve such interests. Other interests, such as ensuring that the United States has secure access to oil and strategic minerals such as strontium, and resolving drug and immigration problems are also important, as are Mexico's recent concerns about cultivating a positive image among the U.S. public.

Ensuring Mexican political stability is an interest both governments share and that motivates a variety of U.S. government programs. A quiet southern flank is important to Washington, not only in bilateral or regional terms but also because a peaceful border makes it easier for the United States to project its power elsewhere. Washington also wants to make sure that Mexico's economic reforms get fully implemented, a condition that requires compliance from the Mexican public and the continued strength of neoliberal forces in the Mexican government. Moreover, Washington sees Mexico not only as an important neighbor but also as a door to the rest of Latin America. Aligned with the United States both economically and politically, Mexico serves as a buffer from the poverty and radicalism that have characterized much of Latin America.[12]

Likewise, political stability and maintaining the dominant position of the PRI are two major interests of the Mexican government that are served by current U.S.-Mexico relations. The legitimacy of the PRI government—undermined by widespread allegations of election fraud, corruption, abuse of authority, and economic failures—has been severely tested over the last decade. Developing closer relations with the United States, once off limits because of antigringo sentiments, has been one of Salinas' primary strategies for strengthening the PRI's standing in the country. That strategy has allowed the Mexican government to tap into U.S. programs and assistance packages that have helped Mexico sort its way out of its economic crisis and recoup some lost political support among its population.

These other interests aside, the central, overriding issue in official U.S.-Mexico relations is economics. With the exception of Mexican political stability, everything else takes a back seat. All other issues on the bilateral agenda have been subordinated to economic concerns. Mexico has put up with U.S. drug agents on its soil and mounted only pro forma protests when Mexican nationals were kidnapped for trial in the United States on drug charges. Its government has grudgingly accepted U.S. unilateral formulations of immigration policy and has plowed ahead with bilateral discussions even while being bashed by the U.S. Congress and media for corruption and authoritarianism. For its part, the U.S. government has turned its head from ongoing patterns of election rigging and abuse of authority in Mexico. Likewise, despite opposition from U.S. drug and customs authorities because of violence against U.S. drug agents, the executive branch under the Reagan and Bush administrations concluded trade, investment, and debt-management agreements with Mexico that advanced economic integration.

The economic relationship that is emerging between the two countries is the product of many forces. Corporate and financial sectors that stand to gain from exploiting cheap Mexican labor and enhanced trade and investment opportunities have strongly influenced the specific features of NAFTA and other economic agreements. The vast majority of the members of the Advisory Committee on Trade Policy and Negotiations, for example—created to give private citizens an advisory role in trade negotiations—are representatives of Fortune 500 corporations. But the self-interest of some sectors of the U.S.

economic elite is only one factor shaping integration. Both countries also have real economic needs that they hope to satisfy, at least in part, through increased economic integration.

Placing its bets on expanding trade and foreign investment in order to finance major portions of the country's "modernization," the Mexican government turned to the United States, its major trading partner. In a speech to the U.S. Congress in 1989 President Salinas explained the government's perspective: "In order for Mexico's modernization to be lasting, we must grow; but growth requires greater and more secure access to the world's largest market, the United States."[13] Ensuring Mexico's access to the U.S. market is not enough. A weak and sluggish U.S. economy will not generate enough demand for Mexican products or create the investment dollars needed to galvanize the Mexican economy. Given the country's economic dependence on its northern neighbor, Mexico needs the U.S. economy to be stable, robust, and open.

With the changes in the global economic and political system and a stagnant economy at home, the United States is no longer just the "Colossus of the North." Washington hopes to ensure Mexican economic cooperation partly because of its own need to crank up the domestic economy. In fact, many observers believe the United States is in the throes of national decline.[14] As one expert on U.S. foreign policy explained grimly, "The only light in a dismal economy is the growth of U.S. exports."[15] This very fact means that Washington and the political and economic forces with a stake in the system are moving to shore up U.S. spheres of influence abroad. The improved relationship with Mexico reflects this trend, just as it reflects changes in Mexican attitudes and development strategies that have permitted closer relations with its northern neighbor.

Ever since the end of World War II, when the United States clearly dominated the international economy and had the world's only standing industrial plant, Washington has promoted exports as the main engine of growth in the country. The engine has been sputtering since the 1970s, however, and U.S. policy makers hoped to crank it up by stimulating exports even more. Despite the intensity with which the objective has been pursued, recent U.S. efforts to pump up trade have been stymied by a sluggish international economy plagued by slow growth and recession.[16]

A stagnant global economy means a slowdown in export sales, and given the magnitude of the U.S. need for capital inflows to pay off its debts and refurbish its productive base, the global recession has hit the United States hard. With European integration, German reunification, and increasing economic turmoil in Japan, demand from these traditional trading partners has fallen off. Along with Canada, these regions still purchase the vast majority of U.S. exports, but because their own economies are contracting, their consumers and businesses cannot afford to purchase the quantity of exports needed to pull the United States out of its economic doldrums. In addition, these important U.S. trading partners are increasingly turning to each other to form regional trading blocs. Staying competitive with the European Community and with the Japanese-dominated east Asian bloc is a major reason that the United States has moved to integrate the Western Hemisphere into a free trade area through mechanisms like NAFTA and the Enterprise for the Americas Initiative.[17]

For the United States to maintain its status as a superpower and satisfy the social and employment needs of its people, it must reinvigorate its economy. With the decline in export potential to its traditional trading partners and staying faithful to an export-driven development strategy, Washington has looked south. That fact has drawn the country closer to Mexico.[18] At the end of the NAFTA negotiations, President Bush summarized the administration's hopes: "The Cold War is over. The principal challenge now facing the United States is to compete in a rapidly changing and expanding marketplace. This agreement [NAFTA] will level the North American playing field, allowing American companies to increase sales from Alaska to the Yucatán."[19] But in a sense, mechanisms like NAFTA reflect a "rediscovered Monroe Doctrine," observes one noted analyst, referring to the policy pronounced by President James Monroe warning European powers to forego expansionist ambitions in Latin America.[20] Rather than leveling the playing field, agreements like NAFTA are intended to bias the regional trading game in favor of the United States. By restricting competition from heavyweights like Germany and Japan through the terms of Western Hemisphere free trade agreements, the United States is trying to stake out Latin America as its own economic turf at a time when competition on the world market is increasingly difficult.

In addition to its own economic health, therefore, the United States needs and wants Mexico's economy to be strong and vigorous. Mexico's economic health not only contributes to its own stability, it directly benefits the U.S. economy by providing increased trade and investment opportunities. "A growing economy and increased employment in Mexico," according to former U.S. Ambassador John Negroponte, "translates into a stronger boost to U.S. exports than virtually anywhere else abroad."[21] Policy makers also expect a healthy, stable, and growing Mexican economy to help slash undocumented immigration to the United States. If Mexico can provide enough decent-paying jobs, they argue, the urge to seek work illegally in the United States will be blunted.[22]

Assuring that Mexico continues to liberalize its economy and that current reforms are locked in are other objectives that Washington has pursued in Mexico. If ratified, the free trade agreement would accelerate integration that is already under way but not change the fundamental process itself. More important, from the perspective of its backers, is that a signed free trade accord would seem a guarantee against backsliding for potential investors and traders. NAFTA would assure businesses that future Mexican governments are committed to following the market-oriented policies begun under de la Madrid and Salinas. "Mexico is becoming a showcase" because of its economic reforms, Negroponte maintained. "A NAFTA will help ensure the permanency of these visionary new economic directions."[23]

From Conquest to Cooperation

Congratulatory words and joint responses to shared problems are relatively new in U.S.-Mexico relations. A history of conquest and intervention strained relations between the two countries for nearly a century. The annexation of Texas, followed by what Mexicans call the "war of the North American invasion" that cost Mexico almost half its territory, and subsequent U.S. support for political leaders like Porfirio Díaz who would support U.S. territorial and economic claims soured relations. These interventions, with U.S. interference in the Mexican Revolution and the hamhanded arrogance of U.S. corporations in Mexico, left scars on Mexican sovereignty that remained sensitive throughout the society until the late 1980s.[24]

After the Revolution, Washington's direct intervention in Mexico subsided. The Mexican government's institutional stability and its capacity to keep public order satisfied two of Washington's central interests. Except for occasions when the United States thought Mexico trod too heavily on its business interests—as when Lázaro Cárdenas nationalized the country's oil reserves—the two governments mostly maintained an aloof coexistence. Incoming presidents like Dwight Eisenhower pointed to the necessity of improving relations with Mexico, but the issue generally faded in importance as the United States pursued other international concerns like fighting the Vietnam War and standing off against the Soviet Union. As one observer described it, U.S.-Mexico relations went into a "deep freeze" after the Revolution stabilized, until the tensions of mounting problems and increasing interdependence kicked the relationship into a position of top priority decades later.[25]

Aside from conflicts over oil nationalizations in the 1930s and a few drug war-related blips of increased attention in the 1960s, the administration of President Jimmy Carter was the first to act on Mexico's growing importance to the United States. Mexico's discovery of massive oil reserves in the mid-1970s followed close on the heels of a major oil crisis in the United States and preceded another oil shock that hit in 1979. The discovery of new Mexican reserves triggered both hopes and anxieties in Washington. "Mexico," President José López Portillo told Carter in a 1979 meeting, "has suddenly found itself the center of American attention—attention that is a surprising mixture of interest, disdain and fear."[26]

Despite Washington's renewed interest in its southern neighbor, relations were not entirely cordial during Carter's term. Administration high-handedness while negotiating the purchase of Mexican natural gas in 1977, for example, irritated the Mexican government, which burned its surplus fuel rather than sell it to Washington. Personal relations between Carter and López Portillo were so rocky that the Mexican president's foreign minister, Jorge Castañeda, remarked candidly, "I discount the possibility of any sudden, newly discovered or rediscovered good will, sympathy or moral consideration on the part of the United States that could change its attitude toward Mexico. The past history of U.S. policy, its present-day prepotency, its selfishness and conservative mood will not allow for such a change."[27] But Carter and his staff did begin to see Mexico as a mid-level regional power with potential influence over U.S. well-being. His foreign policy team began a top-level review of U.S.-Mexico relations and decided to bring better focus to U.S. policy by setting up a new office of coordinator for Mexican affairs in the Department of State.[28]

The bureaucratic innovations launched under Carter were short-lived. They changed almost immediately under Ronald Reagan, who reintroduced an ad hoc approach to U.S.-Mexico policies. But the objective factors that inspired Carter—growing interdependence and a heightened sense of U.S. vulnerability where Mexico was concerned—colored relations throughout the next decade. For the first year or so after Reagan's election, relations were congenial and optimistic. Flush with oil money and as stable as ever, Mexico seemed like a good bet for protecting U.S. access to oil, stimulating trade, and even smoothing the way with other third world countries.

The collapse of the good times was not long in coming. Mexico's economic crash, bank nationalizations, and friendly relations with Central American revolutionary movements in Nicaragua and El Salvador prodded the Reagan administration into a frenzy of activity designed to get Mexico's house in order. Keeping Mexico afloat economically rocketed to the foremost position on the U.S.-Mexico policy agenda. But the Reagan government used Mexico's need for a bailout to push for its own objectives in political as well as economic spheres, and Mexico's compounded economic and political troubles provided more leeway for direct U.S. intervention than had been available for years. In the words of one expert, "A heightened sense of invincibility and moral superiority on the part of the United States contrasted sharply with a deepening sense of vulnerability and social decay in Mexico."[29]

Even with the sharp edge of asymmetric power so evident during these years, Mexico's concessions to U.S. desires did not come easily. Mexico's prickly independence and the complicated structural origins of many of the problems that most concerned Washington defied both easy solutions and ready compliance with the U.S. agenda. As the problems of drug trafficking, burgeoning Mexican migration, and Mexican authoritarianism were added to the list of Washington's dissatisfactions with Mexico, the relationship spiraled downward. Likewise, Mexico's participation in multilateral third world bodies, like the Contadora group, that were trying to reach a negotiated solution in Central America irked the

Reagan administration, which was then supporting military ac-
tions in the region.[30] With all these points of contention, the two
countries roller-coastered through the mid-1980s.

Behind all the public hubbub, however, financial policy makers in the two countries were hard at work on debt, trade, and
other economic issues. Mexico's announcement in August 1982
that it could not meet its international financial obligations sent
shock waves throughout U.S. and global financial communities.
Rather than let the Mexican ship of state sink—an event that
would have towed under U.S. banks and destabilized the global
economy—a team of U.S. government officials and private bank
leaders organized a bailout that helped Mexico over the worst of
the crisis.[31] Other packages worked out in 1986 and 1989 under
the so-called Baker and Brady plans (named after the U.S. secre-
taries of the treasury who proposed them) also helped Mexico
manage its debt obligations. These packages provided Mexico with
a combination of new money, credits, and lengthier repayment
periods on old loans. Under all three plans, Mexico was required
to implement free market strategies, such as liberalizing trade,
selling off government enterprises, devaluing the peso, and
shrinking government spending. The process meant that U.S. and
other foreign financial leaders gained more and more influence
over Mexico's economic policies, inspiring one critic to blast the
"dizzying process of denationalization of the decision-making ap-
paratus for economic policy."[32]

More than Mexico's economic policy was being targeted by the
United States during these years. Mexico's financial troubles lifted
some spirits in U.S. policy-making circles, hopeful that Mexico's
concessions on economic issues would spin off into other policy
areas. "With the wind out of its sails, Mexico is likely to be less
adventuresome in its foreign policy and less critical of ours," predicted a confidential memorandum of the Department of State's
Office of Inter-American Affairs in the early 1980s.[33] A secret
presidential directive signed in 1984 authorized U.S. officials to
pressure the Mexican government to get on board with U.S. initiatives in Central America.[34] By the end of the decade, the early
hopes of U.S. policy makers seemed close to realization. After Salinas first called for the negotiation of a free trade pact, Ambassador Negroponte cabled Washington that the agreement would

"institutionalize [Mexican] acceptance of a North American orientation to Mexico's foreign relations."[35]

As Mexico plodded into alignment with U.S. foreign policy, it was moving much more rapidly into a partnership on trade and investment that laid the foundation for current U.S.-Mexico relations. A bilateral subsidies code signed in 1985 gave Mexico greater access to the U.S. market in exchange for Mexico's phasing out its export subsidies. Along with other changes Mexico was making in its economy, the agreement helped lay the groundwork for Mexico's entry into the GATT the following year. By 1987, the two countries had signed a Bilateral Trade and Investment Framework Understanding that provided the most comprehensive and flexible mechanism to that time for enhancing trade and investment relations. Opening the doors even further, in 1989 the United States and Mexico signed an agreement on "trade and investment facilitation." In going beyond the voluntary provisions of the 1987 framework understanding to mandate negotiations on bilateral trade and investment, the new agreement was the last major stepping stone to NAFTA.

By the end of 1989 the two governments were increasingly acting as if they were engaged in a "special relationship" with reconcilable, if not common, objectives.[36] Reaching such a point required profound adjustments in Mexico's usual nationalistic approach to the United States. Whether the relaxation of nationalist rhetoric will hold over the long term—especially as the presence of foreign business and the U.S. government increases in the country—is unclear. But along with Washington, the Salinas government has been careful to stay focused on what the two governments have defined as their top priority: the rapid integration of their economies. In the process, they are underlining the points on which they agree, while minimizing the differences.

Model for the Hemisphere

As Mexico gradually moved from the back burner to the forefront of U.S. policy concerns, Washington took a new top-level approach to bilateral relations. It was not that Mexico eclipsed other U.S. foreign policy concerns, but rather that its importance as a key player in regional economic integration was recognized by U.S. policy makers and private sector free traders. Mexico, as a bridge between North and South in the hemisphere, was increasingly seen as a model not only for other potential bilateral trade and investment agreements, but for emerging relationships between industrialized countries and mid-level developing countries. Speaking of the proposed U.S.-Mexico free trade agreement, an American trade official observed, "It's possible this could be a prototype arrangement between an industrial and a developing country."[37]

Working out a satisfactory trade and investment regime with Mexico was seen by U.S. policy makers as the first link in a chain of bilateral agreements with other governments in Latin America. The Bush administration intended these bilateral agreements to act as stepping stones to a hemisphere-wide free trade arrangement and to advance the goals of the Enterprise for the Americas Initiative. Enhancing economic ties with the United States was only one objective of initiatives like these. Washington also expected them to strengthen U.S. positions in international trade negotiations and to help lock in the neoliberal economic reforms implemented during the 1980s by governments in the region. With the second largest economy in Latin America and as the major trading partner of the United States in the region, Mexico served as a significant model of the neoliberal strategy of development. NAFTA, according to Bernard Aronson, assistant secretary of state for inter-American affairs under Bush, gave "momentum to the entire hemisphere's drive to lower trade barriers."[38]

Mexico's status as a model had political roots as well. The country's standing as a critic of U.S. interventionism and its efforts to carve out economic and foreign policies independent of the United States gave its new pro-U.S. tilt added weight in Latin America. Likewise, the government's decision to abandon import-substituting industrialization strategies and inwardly focused development policies in favor of closer links to the United States and the world market had more than just domestic significance. Moves like these implicitly challenged dependency explanations of underdevelopment and state-driven development strategies common in Latin America.[39]

Mexico was not the first Latin American nation to make these changes—Chile under Augusto Pinochet was the pioneer. But when Mexico hitched its wagon to the U.S. star, the decision reverberated throughout Latin America: The country's proximity to the region's largest market threatened the export potential of other Latin American countries that were following export-driven growth strategies. Concerns that Mexico would edge out their products in the U.S. market led other Latin American governments to move toward similarly close ties with the United States.[40] Along with a general neoliberal trend evident in the 1980s, these concerns helped advance the U.S. objective of extending its own economic influence in the region.

In addition to serving as a model for regional and North-South relationships, Mexico and NAFTA play important roles in Washington's global economic strategies. In a cable outlining "Talking Points on NAFTA" for U.S. consulates, Ambassador Negroponte explained the tactic: "A vibrant North American partnership for open trade and investment greatly strengthens our leverage in fostering an open global economy to counter the troubling tendencies towards regionalism in Europe and Asia."[41] The change of administrations in Washington is unlikely to affect goals like these. Although President Clinton must focus more on domestic economic needs because of the concerns of his constituency, he will still be driven by economic necessity to push for open trading regimes that favor U.S. exports.

Whose Agenda?

Among the forces urging the kind of global economic integration sought by Washington are U.S. think tanks and U.S. corporations with interests in Mexico. Through their public relations, lobbying, and educational efforts, both types of organizations have promoted a positive view of the trade pact and of the Mexican government among U.S. policy makers and important interest groups. Some of these organizations have gone well beyond lobbying for NAFTA and other policies that affect U.S.-Mexican relations. They have been incorporated into the policy-making process itself, to the near exclusion of groups that seek more rigorous protections for labor and the environment.

The business organizations that were most influential in the push for NAFTA represented some of the largest transnational corporations in the United States. Many of the associations were ad hoc, formed simply to promote the free trade accord. The Emergency Committee for American Trade and the U.S. Alliance for NAFTA, for example, included members from corporate giants like

American Express and Eastman Kodak, both with major investments in Mexico that are likely to get even more of a boost with the trade agreement. One mega-effort was conducted by the Coalition for Trade Expansion, a lobbying umbrella that included more than 500 corporations and lobbyists from five major trade associations. Representing the Business Roundtable, U.S. Chamber of Commerce, Emergency Committee for American Trade, National Association of Manufacturers, and National Foreign Trade Council, the coalition held weekly strategy sessions to determine how best to press its cause in Congress.[42]

The U.S. Council of the Mexico-U.S. Business Committee conducted a major campaign to see to it that a free trade pact agreeable to U.S. business was negotiated.[43] With more than fifty top corporations as members—including AT&T, Bank of America, Citibank, Coca Cola, and General Motors—the U.S. Council testified to Congress, held forums on the trade talks, and saw itself as a "resource for the U.S. government and the U.S. business community" where bilateral trade negotiations were concerned.[44] It set up committees on areas such as trade and regulation, investment and financial services, and production sharing to devise policy proposals for incorporation into the trade agreement.

The various private sector committees mandated to advise the U.S. trade negotiating team about their needs and concerns under a free trade accord were heavily stacked in favor of large corporate and financial interests. The Advisory Committee on Trade Policy and Negotiations (ACTPN), for example, represents forty-two major corporations but only two labor organizations, the AFL-CIO and the Amalgamated Clothing and Textile Workers Union.[45] Included in ACTPN are top corporations like IBM, Hewlett-Packard, and Dow Chemical. Likewise, the special advisory committees that were set up to advise the NAFTA negotiating team on specific issues vastly overrepresented business in comparison with other sectors. On the committees where environmentalists were included, for example, business members outnumbered environmentalists by about thirty to one.

Although they were not as influential as the business committees, conservative think tanks like the Heritage Foundation and the Center for Strategic and International Studies were tireless supporters of NAFTA. The Heritage Foundation, in fact, has been promoting the notion of a U.S.-Mexico free trade area since the early 1980s. But conservative research and advocacy institutes were not alone in supporting NAFTA and other aspects of U.S.-Mexico economic integration. Study groups at liberal and moderate establishments such as the Inter-American Dialogue, Brookings Institution, and Council on Foreign Relations also explored the issue, generally coming down in favor of the idea of free trade. Through their working groups, conferences, panel discussions, and publications, these institutions helped popularize the trade agreement in key sectors and provided forums for dialogue between policy makers and the private sector.

The agenda promoted by these different entities has served the interests of corporations and banks likely to profit from free trade far more than the interests of working people or the poor. In pursuing this agenda, these business advisory groups and think tanks took an approach similar to that of the U.S. and Mexican governments. Neither Salinas nor Bush sought a trade accord that would compensate those already harmed by rapid integration, much less those who might suffer in the future. Although the Clinton administration may push for somewhat stronger protections for labor and the environment, the strict business focus of the agreement as negotiated excludes most socioeconomic considerations.

Under Bush and Salinas, however, the U.S. and Mexican governments established a package of aid programs that not only advanced economic integration but also threw a temporary safety net under many of the Mexican people who suffered most from the dislocations of restructuring. By siphoning off discontent, these programs allowed the Mexican government to continue liberalizing the economy while helping to maintain stability and the political dominance of the PRI. At the same time, they opened Mexican markets to U.S. exports and promoted trade and investment ties among U.S. and Mexican businesses. Although some aid programs are being cut back under Clinton, most of the programs set up under Bush are being continued, especially those designed to stimulate trade. Such programs—to be explored in the following pages—have furthered the probusiness agenda and shielded both the trade agreement and Mexico's economic reforms from much of the political fallout that might have threatened their survival.

Chapter 1

Boosting Business

The integration of the U.S. and Mexican economies is steaming ahead, propelled by many forces. When U.S. tourists head south for sightseeing and shopping or when Mexican men cross into San Diego to their daily jobs as gardeners, they are helping to blend the economies of the two countries together. Peso devaluations over the past decade have savaged local economies on both sides of the border. *Casas de cambio* dotting the streets in U.S. border communities help Mexican shoppers spend their money in the United States by converting their pesos into dollars. On the Mexican side, currency exchanges are not even necessary for many transactions—dollars will do just fine. Economic integration is proceeding steadily and rapidly, energized by the differences in resources, skills, needs, and desires of people in each country.

Looking only at these everyday linkages, it is easy to assume that integration is occurring strictly as a natural process. But the U.S. and Mexican governments are accelerating and shaping the process, both through the trade and investment agreements discussed previously and through specific programs that promote economic ties. The United States has a distinct advantage over Mexico in these programs. Despite its own economic woes, Washington has many resources at its disposal that it can use as leverage to pry open Mexican markets and chip out a place of dominance for U.S. exports. Working closely with private sector trade associations and national and regional export organizations like the National Peanut Council and the Washington State Apple Commission, U.S. government agencies are making sure that Mexico's liberalization enhances the U.S. economy.

This is not to say that all the efforts to promote economic ties are unilateral. On the contrary, over the past decade the two governments worked more closely together than at any time in recent history to advance commercial relations and investment opportunities. The big changes in the Mexican economy and the Mexican government's decision to shelve anti-U.S. attitudes laid the groundwork for these expanding ties. The Joint Commission on Investment and Trade, for example, and an assortment of binational working groups hammered out many of the details of the changing U.S.-Mexican economic relationship before, during, and after the NAFTA negotiations.[46]

Nor do all economic promotion efforts come solely from the national level. Trade offices run by state governments in the United States are springing up in Mexico. Texas, Illinois, California, Louisiana, Arizona, and New Mexico, for example, have opened offices there, aiming to get more of their state's goods and services sold in Mexico. The value of these ties to state economies can be impressive. California does more trade with Mexico than with the entire European Community. Likewise, Texas conducts nearly $11 billion in trade with Mexico each year.[47]

Washington, however, is the big player in trade and investment promotion. Government agencies offer a full range of export-financing mechanisms and market promotion programs designed to hike U.S. exports to Mexico. Institutions such as the Commodity Credit Corporation (CCC) and the Export-Import Bank (Eximbank) provide lines of credit, loan guarantees, and insurance to take much of the risk out of doing business in Mexico and to give U.S. exporters a competitive edge. At the same time, agencies like the Foreign Agricultural Service (FAS) and the Commerce Department provide insight into the Mexican market and play matchmaker between U.S. businesses and Mexican trade representatives. These agencies sponsor trade shows, conduct trade missions, investigate market trends, and implement various other programs that enhance U.S. export opportunities.

Harvesting Profits

A special target for U.S. export-promotion programs is the market for U.S. agricultural products. The restructuring of Mexico's agricultural sector and the government's efforts to cut away trade barriers threw open the door to imports from the United States. As a result, U.S. agricultural exports to Mexico more than doubled after the mid-1980s, climbing to nearly $3 billion in 1991 and to $3.5 billion in 1992.[48] According to Wendell Dennis, an economist at the Foreign Agricultural Service, the growth in U.S. agricultural exports to Mexico is "unprecedented" and the number of new U.S. industry groups looking into doing business in the country is "overwhelming."[49] The trend has not diminished under the Clinton administration. Dennis said that agricultural trade with Mexico has "heated up much more than expected" in the last year, with estimates on trade levels being exceeded in 1992 and the same expected in 1993.[50] Mexico is the third largest customer for U.S. agricultural goods, and U.S. export-promotion programs are designed to boost sales of everything from lunchmeat to table eggs, feed grains, and beef.[51]

The Export Enhancement Program (EEP) is one such effort. The EEP is the major U.S. agricultural export subsidy program. Funded by the Commodity Credit Corporation (CCC), the program awards cash bonuses to U.S. agricultural producers, processors, and exporters so they can offer lower prices on the world's markets for their products. The EEP is a subsidy program that is intended to counteract the agricultural subsidies of other governments, especially those of the European Community, whose farm products often compete directly with those of the United States in global markets.[52] As with NAFTA, programs like the EEP are also designed to increase U.S. clout in multilateral trade negotiations. Wendell Dennis explained that the EEP is "our leverage against unfair trade practices," especially by other GATT members. One of the main objectives of the program, according to the Department of Agriculture, is to "encourage other countries exporting agricultural commodities to undertake serious negotiations on agricultural trade problems."[53]

But the EEP provides more mundane benefits as well. Combined with other U.S. government economic promotion programs, it helps U.S. businesses sew up parts of the Mexican market. In Mexico the program is not especially large in dollar terms, but it did help the United States beat out its competitors in the Mexican wheat market. From 1988 to 1990 wheat was the crop most subsidized under the EEP in Mexico, providing a big boost to U.S. producers, especially when other U.S. government supports were factored into the equation.[54] Subsidies from the program, along with U.S. government credit guarantees, allowed the United States to capture a full 95 percent of the Mexican market for wheat in

1989-1990.[55] Other products supported by EEP subsidies have included vegetable oil and canned peaches, although barley malt is the major commodity promoted under the program as of this writing.[56] In addition to the EEP, U.S. export subsidy programs focusing on dairy, sunflower seed oil, and cottonseed oil products are active in Mexico.[57] As contradictory as it seems, these subsidies will not be affected by NAFTA. The negotiators wrote into the agreement explicit protection for the programs.[58]

Those who profit from the EEP are not the hard-pressed "family farms" that politicians in the United States embrace in speeches and media appearances. On the contrary, large transnational companies benefit most. During the big wheat push of the late 1980s, for example, huge grain producers and exporters like Cargill, Continental Grain, and ADM took the greatest advantage of the program.[59] Like these heavyweights, the Mexican government has benefited from the program. The government's basic-foods distributor, Conasupo, was the largest user of the EEP in Mexico at least until the late 1980s.[60] Because of the country's economic reforms, more private sector buyers began to participate in the program. But Conasupo's strong participation in this and other U.S. export-promotion programs allowed the Mexican government to continue providing inexpensive food even in the face of social service cutbacks. Through programs like these, U.S. taxpayers in effect help pay for the export operations of transnational agribusiness, as well as some of the social costs of Mexico's economic liberalization.

Subsidies like the EEP are only one component of a package of U.S. government export-promotion initiatives that include market development programs and credit guarantees. The strategy is simple: Subsidies keep the prices of U.S. exports competitive, while market development programs help ensure that there is a receptive market for U.S. businesses to penetrate, and credit guarantees make financing easier to come by.

The Market Promotion Program (MPP) and the Foreign Market Development program (FMD), for example, help U.S. businesses stir up interest in Mexico for products they want to export to the country. These programs use funds from the CCC to help pay the costs of U.S. producers and exporters for some of their market development activities in targeted countries.[61] The FMD helps U.S. businesses provide technical assistance and trade services—like training seminars, demonstration farms, and roving marketing representatives who solicit new business and promote new products.[62]

Focusing more on direct advertising of products is the MPP—known until 1990 as the Target Export Assistance (TEA) program. Through the MPP, U.S. businesses can get support for everything from radio jingles, to television commercials, to food fairs.[63] On a global basis, programs like these are being cut back, but in Mexico they are expanding. The U.S. government spent $1.2 million on these programs in 1988, climbing to $2.7 million in 1990, a trend that is expected to continue.[64]

"Without the MPP," according to Wendell Dennis of FAS, "we wouldn't be able to achieve the level of exports we have in the world."[65] Mexico is no exception, although because it is a relatively new market under the MPP, there are little data to show how effective the promotions have been. But Dennis attributes at least some of the sharp increase in U.S. commodity exports to Mexico to the effects of the MPP. If NAFTA is ratified, the program will play an even stronger role because the trade agreement would open up so many new areas to U.S. access. High-value and consumer-ready U.S. exports like breakfast foods, snack items, frozen foods, table eggs, meat, poultry, and microwave foods will be able to enter Mexico more freely. MPP will play a strong role in convincing Mexican consumers that these products are just what they need and in influencing Mexican retailers to stock up on these U.S. products.

Providing the biggest boost for U.S. agricultural exports to Mexico are the GSM (general sales manager) credit guarantees of the U.S. Department of Agriculture (USDA). As with other government insurance and guarantee programs, GSM programs reduce the risk to business and the U.S. banking community of operations in Mexico. Through GSM, the U.S. Department of Agriculture underwrites letters of credit issued by Mexican banks to Mexican buyers of imports from the United States. By providing guaranteed repayment in case of default by the Mexican importer or bank, the GSM programs help protect U.S. exporters and the U.S. banks involved in the transactions. Since Mexico's external debt is still large enough to make U.S. banks skittish about lending even more money to Mexican buyers, the program is instrumental in keeping U.S. export sales climbing in Mexico. Both the Mexican government and commercial importers are able to get the cash they need to buy U.S. agricultural products because of the GSM programs. At the same time, U.S. financial institutions are guaranteed repayment at commercial rates of interest—all thanks to U.S. taxpayers.

Mexico is the world's largest beneficiary of these credit guarantees. The country's use of the GSM programs jumped from $38 million in 1982 to $1.2 billion in 1988, reflecting the country's dramatic opening to U.S. exports, as well as Conasupo's rising purchases of corn.[66] Most of these transactions are covered under GSM-102, whose repayment terms range from six months to three years.[67] In recent years, Mexico has used more than one-fifth of the total allocation for GSM-102 credit guarantees worldwide. In fiscal year 1992, for example, some $1.3 billion in GSM-102 credit guarantees were used by Mexico, covering more than twenty commodity lines.[68] Another $1.45 billion in credit guarantees has been allocated for 1993.[69] Most of the GSM-102 guarantees have traditionally covered bulk commodities like corn, coarse grains, oilseeds, and wheat. The recent increased interest in high-value and consumer-ready products, however, has stimulated sales of such products as meats, hides and skins, table eggs, and nonfat dry milk.[70] To give an idea of the magnitude of this assistance, USDA guarantee programs cover $40 million worth of meat exports to Mexico out of a total of $100 million in such exports.[71]

Programs like these represent a boon to U.S. transnationals and banking institutions by allowing Mexican buyers to purchase U.S. agricultural products they might otherwise be unable to afford. Since Mexico needs many of these products—the country no longer produces enough corn to feed its people, for instance—the programs seem like a win-win proposition. But they have a dark underside as well. The U.S.-backed shift to export-oriented agricultural production in Mexico has widened the gap between the country's need for foodstuffs like corn and the agricultural sector's ability to meet that need. By filling the gap with low-cost U.S. products subsidized by the U.S. taxpayer, Washington has helped the Mexican government compensate for some of the immediate ill effects of restructuring the agricultural sector.

At the same time, however, these programs help to undercut domestic production of basic foods in Mexico and remove incentives for devising policies to achieve food self-sufficiency. They also increase Mexico's dependence on U.S. sources for food and agricultural inputs like feed for livestock. Moreover, they provide only a temporary safety net that must be held in place by an increase in Mexico's debt obligations to the United States. If Mexico loses out on its gamble that liberal economic reforms will launch a new period of dynamic growth—that is, if enough jobs are not created for displaced workers and if exports cannot provide the foreign exchange to pay for increased dependence on U.S. agribusiness—the safety net will come crashing down amid the notes due to U.S. creditors.

These programs—and the reliance on the United States that they encourage—pose other potential dangers for Mexico. In the case of products that are not normal fare in Mexico—such as high-priced and specialty items like beef and microwaveable foods—U.S. export-promotion programs are helping to transform the Mexican market so that it complements the needs of U.S. suppliers. Turning toward the United States for such products enhances the economic prospects of some U.S. agribusinesses and of the Mexican and U.S. retail stores that can capitalize on changing tastes in the country. But over the long haul, these policies are likely to make Mexico more economically and culturally dependent on its northern neighbor—especially if consumption is artificially stimulated by U.S. credit and market-development programs.

Some of these programs are influencing a shift in Mexican production strategies with untold consequences. For example, the U.S. Feed Grains Council, a private sector trade association that participates in many USDA programs, is using U.S. government funding to promote the use of feedlots in the Mexican beef industry. Aside from helping to pump up sales of U.S. feed grains to Mexico, using feedlots represents a shift from Mexico's traditional range-fed approach to raising livestock. Although feedlot use could potentially reduce deforestation and degradation of pastures, it also heightens Mexican dependency on U.S. feed grain technology and supplies, which in turn are highly dependent on petroleum-based products and processes during production.

What is most striking about such business promotion programs is the fact that they appear to contradict the neoliberal agenda pursued by conservative administrations in Washington over the last decade. While these administrations pushed countries like Mexico to remove government supports for local businesses, they made sure that U.S. government programs bolstered and protected large U.S. exporters. These programs were not, however, just the products of trade-oriented Republican administrations. Programs like the EEP and MPP were promoted in part by the Democratic-controlled Congress in response to the competitive problems faced by U.S. agricultural enterprises. All indications are that they will continue and expand under Clinton.

Financing the Trade Explosion

Far more than just U.S. agricultural products are promoted in Mexico through U.S. programs. The explosion of exports to Mexico in services, retail and capital goods, and high technology was ignited not only by Mexico's economic liberalization, but also by Washington's trade promotion programs. Virtually every facet of the Mexican economy is a target for such promotions. From the Commerce Department's matchmaker and research services, to the Trade and Development Program's funding for feasibility studies, to the export-financing services of Eximbank, the U.S. government is helping U.S. businesses carve out market shares in sectors as wide-ranging as petrochemicals, insurance, and environmental protection.[72]

Mexico's own development objectives influence the kinds of goods and services that receive top promotion. An example is the environmental sector. Mexico's plans to step up environmental protection and clean up the country's air, water, and soil caught the attention—and the promotion budgets—of several government and nongovernmental agencies in the United States. Helping draw that attention were huge loans from the World Bank—still heavily influenced by the U.S. vote—and untied credits from Japan designated for environmental projects.[73] Responding to factors like these, the U.S.-Mexico Joint Committee for Investment and Trade identified Mexico's environmental and pollution control sectors as top priorities in terms of trade and investment opportunities. The Commerce Department's International Trade Administration sponsored trade missions, published articles in business journals, and provided information and other assistance to U.S. exporters hoping to take part in the sales boom. Newly formed institutions like the Environmental Technology Export Council—a partnership of U.S. corporations, national laboratories, and trade associations—set their sights on Mexico as a gold mine of export opportunity in the field.

Helping to make sure that export opportunities do not get lost to foreign competitors is the U.S. Export-Import Bank. Eximbank is the principal export financing arm of the U.S. government, and its programs have been instrumental in keeping binational trade thriving. Eximbank's services are offered in some 155 countries, but Mexico by far the favored beneficiary. This position is not surprising, given Mexico's status as the United States' third largest trading partner. Even with that status, however, the share of Eximbank funding that goes to Mexico is remarkable. In 1992, for example, more than 25 percent of the bank's portfolio was devoted to backing sales of U.S. goods and services to Mexico although the country accounts for only 7 percent of U.S. trade.[74] The bank supports U.S. exports to Mexico under all of its programs: direct loans to foreign buyers, intermediate credits to U.S. lending institutions, loan guarantees, and export credit insurance. Available to both public and private buyers, these services protect U.S. banks and businesses from risk, while offering loans at the lowest rates possible under international agreements.[75]

Protecting U.S. corporations from many of the risks that are normal by-products of doing business abroad is a major reason Eximbank exists. Loan guarantees, for example, mean the U.S. taxpayer will foot the bill if the buyer or Mexican bank defaults. Similarly, Eximbank's insurance programs protect businesses from both political and other noncommercial risks for a reasonable premium. "By neutralizing the effect of export credit subsidies from other governments and by absorbing risks that the private sector will not accept," the bank explains, "Eximbank enables U.S. exporters to compete effectively in overseas markets."[76] That objective has certainly been met in Mexico, where Eximbank has been active since 1946. The amount designated for Mexico expands or contracts depending on the state of the Mexican economy, with Mexico's trade liberalization sparking a whopping increase. From 1946 to 1990, for example, Mexico received more than $3 billion in Eximbank loans and credits.[77] Within two short years, though, Mexico's outstanding loans and credits with the bank had more than doubled, climbing to $7.5 billion by the end of 1992.[78] As of 1993, the total was $8.2 billion.[79]

The bank's services have covered nearly every sector of the Mexican economy, from telecommunications, to aviation, to construction and power. Working with Nafinsa, the Mexican govern-

ment's business development bank, Eximbank developed a guarantee program to support the privatization and modernization of
Mexico's agroindustry and electronics sectors.[80] The bank's services are also available to support Mexican purchases of U.S. antidrug defense items.

Over the years, Eximbank has helped U.S. companies like
General Electric, Beech Aircraft Corporation, and the Fuller Company hike their exports to Mexico. Many of these sales—especially
of goods like locomotives and railway equipment, aircraft, and inputs for Mexico's cement industries—not only provide short-term
profits for U.S. exporters but also strengthen the infrastructure
and competitive standing of Mexican companies. Some of the largest conglomerates in the Mexican cement industry, for example,
have become so successful that they are now competing in the
United States.[81]

The most controversial Eximbank programs among Mexicans
involve support for transactions involving Mexico's petroleum sector.[82] Washington's support for Mexico's oil industry has payoffs in
terms of the U.S. need for dependable oil supplies and Mexico's interests in modernizing the industry and developing new oil fields. But
U.S. involvement in this sector concerns Mexicans worried about
losing control over the country's valuable reserves. More than half
its annual petroleum exports are sold to U.S. oil companies, and for
several years in the 1980s Mexico was the largest contributor to the
U.S. Strategic Petroleum Reserve.[83] Considering the country's proximity to the United States and the size of its reserves, helping Mexico
expand exploration and development of its oil supplies is a vital interest that Washington is meeting with programs like these. As of
late 1992 the United States seemed well on its way to assuring secure access to Mexican oil. By that time, about 20 percent of Eximbank's Mexican loan portfolio was tied up with loans to Pemex,
Mexico's state-owned oil giant.[84]

Trade, Aid, and Runaways

Just as government export-financing programs foster U.S. exports to Mexico, so do other U.S. programs make it easier for U.S.
corporations to do business in Mexico or set up shop in the country. By financing feasibility studies, training, research studies,
conferences, and other needs, the development assistance of the

U.S. Agency for International Development (AID) may well be encouraging some U.S. businesses to relocate to Mexico. It is not that promoting runaways is an explicit objective of the agency. Rather, the types of services that AID funds to make maquiladoras and other targets of foreign investment more profitable and productive often attract U.S. corporations that may or may not already be considering a southward move.[85] The issue points out a dilemma faced by U.S. aid policies as the economy globalizes: Boosting development in poor countries often means helping foreign exports and low-wage workers compete against U.S. products and workers, a particularly troublesome reality in a declining economy.

This fact prompts periodic outbursts in Congress and the media. Sensitivities in AID about the issue of stimulating foreign competition with foreign assistance run so hot that when Arthur Danart of AID's Mexico desk was asked about the agency's trade promotion programs, he responded, "I choose not to answer." AID, he noted, had been receiving adverse publicity in the previous weeks about just such concerns, leading Congress to tighten its restrictions. In fact, legislation that prohibited using congressional appropriations to lure U.S. businesses to set up operations outside the United States was first written as early as 1986.[86]

The practice of providing services *useful* to such businesses has continued, however. It is defended by AID officials as a boon to Mexican development and by members of other U.S. commerce and trade agencies as a prudent intervention designed to keep U.S. plants from moving even farther offshore.[87] If they move to Mexico instead, the argument goes, then more jobs are saved in the United States that would otherwise be shipped abroad to foreign suppliers, transportation companies, services, and other such links in the production process.

Up to $2 million was allocated by AID in 1992 to promote U.S.-Mexico trade and investment.[88] The money was used to help build infrastructure needed for these activities, as well as to transfer know-how and equipment to Mexican recipients. In one program, for example, AID funded the Technological Institute of Higher Education in Monterrey (ITESM) to show Mexican shrimpers how to construct, install, and use turtle excluder devices (TEDs) in their fleets. Because they were catching too many protected sea turtles in their nets, their shrimp was not allowed access to the U.S. market. By using the TEDs, however, they would be able to sell their catch in the United States.

Likewise, some of the research studies funded by AID are designed to solve problems faced by U.S. businesses in Mexico, especially the maquiladoras. Working with business organizations like the American Chamber of Commerce in Mexico and the Mexico-U.S. Business Committee, AID grantees identify problem areas and explore potential solutions. One AID-funded study, conducted by the University of the Americas, investigated the problem of high employee turnover in the plants, looking at issues like unionism, wages, housing, and working conditions.[89] In another case, AID financed a survey of industries in Mexico to find out what kinds of technical skills were needed by employees. This information was then used by Mexican technical training schools to design curricula to meet those needs.[90]

Another research project planned by AID looked at the feasibility of creating maquiladora industries in various parts of the Mexican interior.[91] Once again, this study reflects the North-South contradictions that exist between long-term Mexican and U.S. interests. Since most of the maquilas are owned by U.S. enterprises, this kind of program is clearly in danger of promoting plants that run away to Mexico. On the other hand, expanding the number of maquilas in the Mexican interior might indeed reduce population and environmental pressures on the border and help stimulate the Mexican economy through wages and backward linkages.

Other AID programs besides research studies are intended to help solve the problems of businesses in Mexico—whether owned by Mexicans or by U.S. companies. AID's 1991-92 Action Plan for Mexico noted that "the lack of adequate housing and infrastructure" was a big reason the maquiladoras had trouble retaining employees. Although not offering to subsidize housing or "other amenities," AID proposed to put together a technical assistance and training package to help the construction, business, and banking communities meet the needs of maquila communities in terms of housing and infrastructure.

AID's recent budgets in Mexico have included funding for trade promotion and implementation of NAFTA, even though the agreement has not been ratified. For example, the agency sponsored a three-day business development conference in Austin, Texas, which included business leaders interested in expanding cross-border trade.[92] In another case, an AID-funded study looked at regional infrastructure, characteristics of local labor, and commercial and educational facilities so that potential investors would know where the best opportunities lay for investment.[93]

The agency also worked to get NAFTA provisions carried out, even before the trade agreement was signed by Bush and Salinas. Gerard Bowers, AID's representative in Mexico City under Bush, said that "one of AID's roles here [in Mexico] is not only to make sure that NAFTA's passed but also to make sure of its implemented success."[94] These AID programs aim to achieve compatibility between NAFTA and the regulations, standards, and day-to-day operations of Mexican businesses and government agencies. In the case of intellectual property rights, for example, AID worked with the Mexican Ministry of Trade and Industrial Development (SECOFI) to install new regulations for copyrights and other such protections. It also funded training for Mexican businesses to set up and operate environmental protection devices to meet NAFTA standards.

Taking Aim at the U.S. Market

Mexico has a few of its own programs designed to expand business ties with the United States. Although these initiatives are part of Mexico's attempt to win a bigger piece of the economic pie for its own industries, they are dwarfed in size and scope by U.S. programs. Given the other disparities in the relationship, Mexico's chances of vastly enlarging its market in the United States are unsure. But many of these programs are also designed to attract U.S. investment to Mexico, one of the country's main objectives as its economy opens up. That objective will more likely be fulfilled—not just because of these efforts, by any means, although they are important for providing information about markets, policies, and trade services. Whether Mexican businesses will be able to stand up against the greater resources of the U.S. competitors attracted to the country with such programs is far less clear.

The country's foreign trade bank, Bancomext, provides funding for infrastructure development and other projects that support Mexican exports and joint ventures with foreign businesses. As with some U.S. government programs, the infrastructure that is developed sometimes crosses the line between the two countries.

In one case, Bancomext put up a $105 million loan to finance construction of the McAllen Produce Terminal Market in McAllen, Texas. When completed, the market will warehouse Mexican agricultural products for sale in the United States.[95] Similarly, the national finance bank, Nafinsa, set up a special loan fund to help finance joint ventures by companies in Mexico and U.S. businesses owned by Latinos.[96]

Aside from financial support, government programs in Mexico provide other services to stimulate trade and investment relations. In Mexico City, the Exports Promotion Commission (Compex) helps small- and medium-size would-be exporters get loans from Bancomext and Nafinsa and find market niches in the United States. Compex, launched in early 1992 by the municipal government of Mexico City, focuses mostly on the assembly sector, such as appliances, shoes, and dressmaking, but it also promotes other industries, such as chocolate producers and flower growers. In addition to promoting exports, projects like Compex are intended to offset some of the negative effects of economic restructuring. According to Compex director Gina Dalma, "A lot of the smaller industries were being left out" when the economy began to pick up in the late 1980s. "Compex came about as an attempt to help them participate in the opening up of the economy," Dalma explains. "No company will survive long these days if it isn't an exporter."[97]

On a national scale, the Trade Commission of Mexico provides information and matchmaker services. With offices in major cities across the United States, the government-sponsored commission helps businesses in the United States and Mexico find trading or investment partners in the other country. Ironically, the majority of the services offered by the commission seem designed to move U.S. enterprises into Mexico, as opposed to promoting Mexico's exports in the United States. Of the seven major types of information services provided by the commission, five are specifically aimed at attracting U.S. investment or exports. Companies can find out how to set up a maquila along the border or how to go about getting products made or assembled in Mexico. Details about what opportunities are available in specific regions of the country can also be obtained from the commission, as can information about market development activities like trade shows. In fact, these are some of the same types of services offered by the U.S. Commerce Department. With both the Mexican and U.S. governments working to expand export and investment options for U.S. businesses, it is no wonder that trade and investment relations surged in the past few years and that economic integration has advanced so quickly.

Chapter 2

Development, Democracy, and the Drug War

Programs designed to boost trade and investment ties between the United States and Mexico do not stand alone. Other U.S. and Mexican programs are designed to respond to such issues as drug trafficking, political liberalization, and the needs of Mexicans dislocated by economic reforms. These programs have not received as much funding in overall terms as those intended to stimulate economic ties. Nonetheless, they have helped in crucial ways to underpin the economic policies of the Mexican government, while enhancing the image of that government and extending the influence of the United States.

Information and exchange programs have drawn the two countries closer together, providing a common pool of knowledge and skills in fields like trade relations, drug control, and environmental regulation. United States development assistance, food aid, and military assistance have been used to spawn links among counterparts in each country, promote Mexico's development agenda, and protect the PRI from the political fallout resulting from restructuring. In addition, U.S. democratization programs, though far more modest in Mexico than in many other developing countries, have helped to spread free-market beliefs and supported the efforts of some civic groups trying to make the Mexican political system more competitive.

Wooing the Public

In a democracy, even imperfect democracies like those in Mexico and the United States, generating public support for government initiatives is essential. The interest groups and social sectors that the U.S. and Mexican governments woo on behalf of initiatives like NAFTA or border environmental programs are the same voters who can vote thumbs up or down on election candidates and, in many cases, on their pet projects.

Washington courts the Mexican public to some extent—mostly through visitor delegations and conferences—but political differences between the two countries make that task less essential than Mexico's courtship of U.S. social and political forces. The Mexican system is far more centralized and is still subject more to the wishes and aims of the PRI than to any other social force. By making direct appeals to the most powerful decision makers in the party and in its core constituencies, the U.S. government can rather easily make its case.[98]

In contrast, the U.S. political system has thousands of vulnerable points of influence that can make or break a piece of legislation or dramatically change the content of proposed laws, regulations, or international agreements. Convince a congressional committee chair or his or her top staffer to oppose a particular proposal, for instance, and the initiative is well on its way to the trash heap. Hiring former U.S. government officials as consultants means back-door entry to executive branch offices, as well as insight on the best way to run the bureaucratic gauntlet. Similarly, generating a political constituency—say, in business or ethnic communities, or in the labor or environmental sectors—means domestic political pressure will be applied to elected U.S. officials.

Hoping to assure NAFTA's passage and secure access to the U.S. market, the Mexican government concentrated on countering U.S. backlash against the trade accord and fears about economic interdependence and job loss. In an effort to improve its image in the United States, Mexico opened a new embassy building in Washington, expanded its staff, and ordered consulates across the United States to promote the free trade pact and reach out to local Mexican Americans. In a highly sophisticated campaign, Mexico hired public relations firms and lobbyists to sell the U.S. public, media, and political leaders on the benefits of initiatives like NAFTA. At the same time, it drafted high-priced U.S. lawyers and consultants to make sure that the country got the best terms possible out of binational deals.

Mexico had conducted some public relations and advertising campaigns in the United States as far back as 1946 under President Miguel Alemán. Until 1990, however, these efforts mostly focused on promoting tourism or the concerns of certain export industries, like cement.[99] By mid-1990 Mexican principals—including government agencies like SECOFI—were beginning to step up their lobbying and public relations activities aimed at U.S. audiences. These efforts really took off in 1991, when the government began hiring some of the most prestigious U.S. firms to press its case in the United States.[100]

Mexico went all out, reportedly spending more than $6 million annually on the effort to sway U.S. opinion (a figure that does not include private sector expenditures).[101] It hired former officials from the U.S. trade representative to consult on trade policy questions, high-powered lawyers to handle tricky trade negotiations, Republican and Democratic lobbying firms, and top-drawer public relations specialists. The burst of activity launched Mexico to the forefront of foreign governments that maintain lobbying and public relations operations in the United States, edging out Japan in the process.

Feeling the heat from environmental and labor opponents of NAFTA, the Mexican government made countering the opposing arguments a top priority. It hired William Brock, for instance, a former secretary of labor and the Office of the U.S. Trade Representative, to consult on the policy and politics of U.S. labor and trade.[102] At the same time, lobbyists like the Republican firms of Gold and Liebengood and Charls E. Walker Associates, as well as the Democratic firms of Public Strategies Washington Inc. and TKC International Inc., pressed Mexico's position in influential congressional committees like the Senate Finance and House Ways and Means committees. TKC, headed by Gabriel Guerra-Mondragon, a former special assistant to the U.S. ambassador to Mexico in the early 1980s, also urged U.S. labor organizations to take another look at the free trade agreement and abandon opposition to the pact.

Enlisted in the campaign were representatives of large corporate interests bound to profit from the free trade accord. Mexico hired Michael B. Smith, a former deputy trade representative, for legal and policy services.[103] Smith heads SJS Advanced Strategies Inc., a unit of the law firm of Steptoe & Johnson. Until mid-1992 he advised a coalition of large Mexican companies about which types of policy proposals might be successful in Washington. Likewise, the Mexican Business Council on Foreign Trade (COECE), an association of Mexican business interests established at the initiative of the Salinas administration, hired Steptoe & Johnson to provide legal and other services that would help the free trade campaign.[104]

Not left out of these efforts were U.S. Latino organizations and Mexican-American communities. Working through consuls in the United States, past Mexican governments had occasionally responded to pleas by Mexican-American organizations like the League for United Latin American Citizens (LULAC) for assistance in their struggles against discrimination. It was not until the Echeverría administration (1970-76), however, that formal ties were developed between Mexico and Mexican-American leaders. Recognizing the mounting political force of Mexican Americans, President Echeverría initiated a series of meetings with the new Chicano leaders of the Southwest. Besides maintaining regular communications, Echeverría and his successor, López Portillo, sponsored scholarship programs for Mexican Americans to attend Mexican universities.[105] Mexico had both ideological and strategic reasons for these new initiatives. Both presidents regarded the Mexican-American community as *el Mexico de afuera* (the other Mexico)—part of the third world that Mexico was purporting to represent in the 1970s. Mexico also viewed the Mexican-American community as the basis of a pro-Mexico lobby in the United States that would bolster its own position in binational negotiations about such issues as immigration, foreign lending, and petroleum sales.[106] The debt crisis and Mexico's move away from third-worldism to neoliberalism resulted in drastic cuts in the scholarship programs and relegated outreach to the Mexican-American leadership to low-priority status during the de la Madrid administration. While some cultural exchange programs continued, the political relations that had been previously cultivated were de-emphasized.[107]

The advent of free trade rekindled Mexican interest in courting the rapidly expanding Latino communities in the United States. In 1990 the Mexican government established the Program for Foreign Mexican Communities under the foreign affairs ministry. A wide-ranging program, it includes outreach in such areas as culture, sports, health, and bilingual education. During its first three years, however, the main thrust of the program has been in the areas of business connections, seminars and exchanges, and political outreach. It has sponsored a Council for Business Promotion with Foreign Mexican Communities and has arranged meetings between Mexican business associations and the local and national Hispanic Chambers of Commerce to promote free trade and U.S. investment in Mexico. Furthermore, the program has renewed scholarship and exchange programs for Mexican-American students and educators as well as cooperated closely with the U.S. Department of Education to meet the "growing education demands of Mexican communities" in the United States. Educational outreach has also included seminars attended by Mexican government officials and Mexican-American leaders and professors.

Under the auspices of this new program the Mexican government has reached out directly to Latino organizations and politicians. Program representatives regularly speak at meetings of the congressional Latino caucus and at the conferences of such groups as the National Council of La Raza, LULAC, Mexican American Legal Defense and Educational Fund (MALDEF), Southwest Voter Education Project, Southwest Voter Research Institute, Mexican American Bar Association, and National Association of Chicano Studies. In addition, the program publishes a tabloid called *La Paloma* from its offices in San Antonio, Texas.[108]

Also part of the new initiative to build alliances with the U.S. Latino populace are high-level, government-sponsored public relations trips to Mexico City to discuss free trade and other bilateral issues. Mirroring such activities are the top-level visits of Mexican officials to the United States to influential sectors of the value of supporting NAFTA and similar ventures. Salinas himself campaigned extensively throughout the United States on NAFTA's behalf. Meeting with the media, environmentalists, congressional representatives, business representatives, and other interest groups, the Mexican president assured them that his country would uphold labor and environmental standards, especially in the heavily industrialized borderlands. He also sought to reassure U.S. labor's fears that jobs would run away to Mexico along with U.S. investment. Without NAFTA, Salinas warned, immigrants from Mexico would continue to cross the border to find jobs in the United States. With NAFTA, he assured, more decent jobs would be created in Mexico, stemming the tide of migration and expanding U.S. export opportunities.

Another part of the Salinas administration's campaign for NAFTA's approval included the hiring of two prominent Mexican-American politicians—Toney Anaya and Jerry Apodaca, both former governors of New Mexico—as registered lobbyists and foreign agents for the Mexican government. Other hired lobbyists included former Navy Secretary Edward Hidalgo and Abelardo Valdez, who served as President Carter's chief of protocol. In its contract with Anaya, the Mexican government's Office for Free Trade Negotiation obligates the Latino leader to, among other things, promote NAFTA among "hispanoamericanos," secure their support for free trade, and see that they pressure their congressional representatives to approve the proposed agreement.

Beginning in 1990, U.S. Latino leaders also became the favored recipients of the Orden Mexicana del Aguila Azteca, the country's highest national honor for foreigners. In the heat of the free trade lobbying campaign, President Salinas awarded the medal to eight Latino leaders for their services to Mexico and humanitarianism. No non-Latino leaders were honored. In the 1990-92 period Salinas presented the decoration to Los Angeles County Supervisor Gloria Molina, National Council of La Raza President Raul Yzaguirre, MALDEF President Antonia Hernández, Chicano community leader Blandina Cárdenas, farmworker organizer Cesar Chavez, and university professors Luis Leal, Julian Samora, and Américo Paredes. During the 1992 awards ceremony, recipients Molina and Yzaguirre were both commended for their efforts to support NAFTA in the United States. Henry Cisneros, another NAFTA supporter, was also nominated for the 1992 Aguila Azteca but could not accept it because of his impending appointment to the Clinton administration.

The strongly favorable response of many leading Latino organizations to NAFTA suggested that the Mexican government's initiatives within the Latino community were not wasted. Such organizations as the National Council of La Raza and the Hispanic Chamber of Commerce jumped on the free trade bandwagon, supporting fast-track negotiating authority and later backing the agreement itself. No major Latino organization joined the early citizen opposition to NAFTA, and most Mexican-American politicians lent their strong support to the agreement. The persistent courtship of the Mexican government gave rise to a curious marriage between such Latino groups as MALDEF and the National Council of La Raza, which defend the rights of Mexicans and Mexican Americans in the United States, and the Mexican government. In their support of free trade, these Latino groups generally made no mention of the pressing issues of human rights violations and economic exploitation of Mexicans in Mexico.[109] The largely supportive positions taken by the national Latino organizations also underlined the class differences that continue to exist between these organizations and the Latino majority.

But courtship by the Mexican government was not the only factor in the early involvement of Latino organizations in the free trade debate. Latino leaders wanted to be players in their own right, and many honestly believed that NAFTA would be mainly beneficial to their communities. The often enthusiastic Latino support for NAFTA arose from the widespread belief that free trade would boost the economies of the border states and open new opportunities for Latino businesspeople and professionals, the sectors that most Latino organizations represented. Economic motives do not, however, fully explain this generally supportive position. Also a factor, especially among Mexican-American leaders, was the perception that the political and economic reforms of the Salinas administration were earning new international respect for Mexico and that this upgraded status would help improve the standing of Latinos in the United States.

As the NAFTA debate evolved, initial Latino support for free trade became more qualified as some Latino leaders came to recognize the possible dangers of economic integration. Business groups such as the Hispanic Chamber of Commerce remained steadfast supporters of the agreement, but other groups began to call for modifications that would address the rising labor, infrastructural, and environmental concerns. The Southwest Voter Research Institute spearheaded a campaign to form a Latino consensus on NAFTA. As the congressional debate on the treaty began in late 1993, the informal coalition of Latino groups mobilized by the institute expressed conditional support for NAFTA. Instead of calling for the renegotiation of the treaty, these groups proposed a set of initiatives and implementing laws that would alleviate the adverse impacts of NAFTA by providing job retraining for displaced workers, increasing funds for border infrastructure, and creating a North American Development Bank.[110]

In the end, the Mexican government's efforts to convene Latino support for what was framed as a foreign policy issue met with only partial success. Like other U.S. social sectors, the Latino community became increasingly concerned that NAFTA was not simply a foreign policy and trade issue but an agreement that could threaten U.S. jobs and economic stability. Cuban-American groups threatened to oppose NAFTA because of Mexico's relations with Cuba, and Puerto Rican organizations expressed their fear that free trade with Mexico would endanger the territory's status as an attractive low-wage export-processing zone.

Informing the Debate

In addition to Mexico's public relations and lobbying campaigns, the U.S. government funds educational, information, and visitor exchange programs targeting Mexico. Offered through a full range of U.S. agencies, including the Commerce Department, AID, Drug Enforcement Administration, Department of Defense, Federal Bureau of Investigation, and U.S. Information Agency (USIA), the programs are designed to create linkages between U.S. and Mexican counterparts, transmit U.S. skills and technology, and promote a positive image of the United States in Mexico. Many of these programs are aimed especially at Mexican leaders in various fields, or at those who, by virtue of education or background, are likely to become leaders in the country.

USIA is the lead agency for conducting these types of programs. In Mexico, USIA generates support for present and proposed U.S. policies through publications, radio and television broadcasts, visitor exchanges, trainings, seminars, and educational opportunities. Over the past few years its major focuses in Mexico have been NAFTA and drug control, although other areas, such as political studies, cultural interchanges, and environmental issues, are also subjects of its programs.

Working with a large number of private organizations and universities, the information agency sponsors visitor exchanges that reach out to a full complement of influential social sectors. Participants include government officials, journalists, educators, artists, youth leaders, athletic coaches, and more. During the negotiations on NAFTA, USIA made sure that a positive view of the proposed accord was promoted both in the United States and in Mexico during visitor exchanges in each country. Participants included nearly everyone with an interest in the topic, ranging from academics, farmers, and government officials, to labor representatives and business leaders. Antinarcotics exchanges are also

common, focusing especially on drug abuse prevention and reha-
bilitation programs.

The agency also produces a number of publications that are
distributed in Mexico, including the Wireless File news service, the
quarterly *Dialogue* (*Facetas*), and *Problems of Communism* (*Problemas
Internacionales*), a bimonthly magazine. Through other publications, its research office reports findings of overseas opinion polls
and other research. Aside from offering interesting information
about the viewpoints of Mexican audiences, these polls help shape
U.S. policy initiatives and indicate whether past policies have
been successful. Recent polls have focused mostly on the drug
war and NAFTA.

Like Mexico's public relations efforts, many of these programs
are devoted to boosting bilateral trade and investment and to carrying the flag for NAFTA. In at least one case, in fact, a USIA
visitor program may well have supported Mexico's lobbying and
public relations activities aimed at the U.S. Congress and influential interest groups. In that instance, USIA sent Lenore Sek, an
analyst and investigator for the Congressional Research Service of
the Library of Congress, on a trip to Hermosillo. There she met
with a PRI representative who is also a prominent state legislator,
head of the PRI's economic think tank, and host of a half-hour
news program dealing with economic issues. Sek described the
U.S. fast-track procedure to the PRI legislator and outlined which
U.S. groups were most likely to support or oppose the free trade
accord.[111] From that meeting Sek went on to have similar discussions with the manager of a U.S.-owned maquiladora and a Mexican college. Whether or not Sek's visit did help Mexico drum up
U.S. support for NAFTA is unclear. That it could have done so,
however, by demystifying the fast-track process and indicating
which groups were lined up for and against it, is certain.

A new binational commission also promotes educational and
cultural ties between the two countries and reflects the growing
mutuality of some aspects of the U.S.-Mexico relationship. The
U.S.-Mexico Commission for Educational and Cultural Exchange
was established following an agreement at the November 1990
summit held by Bush and Salinas in Monterrey. Representing a
top-level commitment to these programs, the commission's ten-
member board is appointed by the Mexican foreign minister and
the U.S. ambassador to Mexico and is evenly divided between

Mexican and U.S. members. The commission is funded by the U.S. and Mexican governments as well as by some private organizations, such as the Rockefeller Foundation.

The commission administers a variety of educational and cultural exchange programs for U.S. and Mexican participants. For example, it administers the Fulbright Scholarship program in Mexico, offering grants for faculty development, English language training, a multidisciplinary master's degree program, and postdoctoral research. The commission's Fund for Culture sponsors small grants (under $25,000) for nonacademic cultural exchanges in fields as diverse as dance, translation, and library management. It also supports nondegree research in cultural scholarship and conferences on cultural themes. With the nonprofit Debt-for-Development Coalition, the commission designed a debt-swap program called "Debt for Science, Technology, and Human Resources" to support research and exchanges between U.S. and Mexican universities.

Despite the commission's binational origins, the United States still dominates the educational effort. This is true not only because the United States is the major source of funding but also because the commission took over programs that used to be administered by USIA. It is still housed in the same building as USIA offices in Mexico City, maintaining direct connections with USIA but operating as a bilateral program.

More than the public relations and lobbying efforts of Mexico aimed at U.S. audiences, these U.S.-dominated information and education programs have the potential to shape the integration of the two countries. Though these exchanges are two-way, favoring a better understanding between the two countries, they are intended to transmit a U.S. way of doing things and seeing the world. Although USIA attempts to achieve diversity in the viewpoints of people chosen for these programs, Mexican and U.S. participants must be selected and approved by USIA and often the U.S. Embassy in Mexico. The result is a blending of the two cultures, but one that is guided in many ways by U.S. government functionaries.

Development Assistance

Mexico is not the top recipient of U.S. development assistance. It is not even in the top tier. With the emphasis on trade, not aid, and with Mexico's economic restructuring winding to a close, development assistance from the United States is declining.[112] In 1992 direct U.S. economic assistance to Mexico totaled $40.6 million, including about $27 million in food aid.[113] In 1993, however, U.S. aid levels dropped to $21 million, and food aid was phased out.[114]

Although current aid levels are being cut, the timing of U.S. assistance in previous years was critical. The assistance that Mexico received beginning in the early 1980s was crucial to the government's "modernization" efforts. Maintaining Mexican stability, underpinning the country's neoliberal reforms, and implementing NAFTA have been central U.S. government interests in Mexico for years, and Washington's development assistance and food aid programs helped advance those objectives. By creating linkages between Mexican institutions and U.S. counterparts, these programs also helped to promote exports of U.S. goods and services. At the same time, by focusing on areas like population control, health services, strengthening the private sector, and global warming, U.S. aid programs responded to concerns shared by the two governments.

Until the 1980s, Mexican nationalist sensitivities were as much an obstacle to increased U.S. aid as the fact that U.S. foreign policy priorities lay elsewhere. Other factors—such as Mexico's relative wealth among developing countries, its overall stability, and political differences between the two countries—also kept aid levels low. From start-up in the mid-1940s until the 1960s, the United States provided an assortment of loans, grants, and food aid programs in the country. Despite the variety, these programs were minimal in dollar terms. From 1962 to 1971, for example, loans and grants from AID totaled only $70 million, the lowest on a per capita basis of any country in Latin America.[115]

Most development aid was cut off by mutual agreement in 1966, in part because Mexico refused to sign a provision guaranteeing U.S. private investment but also because the United States considered Mexico too "rich" to participate in programs designed for poor countries.[116] Mexico's economy was growing steadily at the time, and, according to AID, both governments thought the country would be able to satisfy its technical and financial needs by direct purchase or borrowing.[117] Following the decision, AID closed its offices in Mexico, leaving only a few projects running until they completed their funding cycles in the early 1970s. Over the next years, Washington channeled support for several modest development programs through the government-funded Inter-American Foundation, such international organizations as the United Nations World Food Program, and a few nongovernmental organizations, but official government-to-government aid dried up.

Getting back into the aid business in Mexico was a gradual process. Mexico requested U.S. help on population control programs in 1977, but it took Mexico's economic crisis and subsequent restructuring efforts to revitalize bilateral aid relations. In 1983 significant U.S. assistance began to "fade in again," according to Gerard Bowers, AID's representative in Mexico City during the Bush administration.[118] The agency moved an office into the U.S. Embassy and started food aid and other development assistance programs to ease the impact of the crisis and of the austerity plans being implemented by de la Madrid.[119]

Because AID designates Mexico an advanced developing country (ADC), it did not open a full-scale mission despite widespread poverty and uneven development. In contrast to large, visible operations in other developing countries, the AID office in Mexico maintained a low profile and was run by a bare-bones staff even before the 1993 cutbacks. But Washington funnels aid to Mexico through many other avenues as well. According to Samuel Taylor, who headed AID's Mexico City office in 1989, Mexico has the "largest non-mission program in the world," with "hundreds of projects" being channeled through other government agencies ranging from the Commerce Department to the U.S. Forest Service.[120]

Contributing to the agency's low profile in the country is the fact that most assistance is run through U.S. or Mexican nongovernmental organizations. Organizations like the U.S.-based Northwest Medical Teams, the Mexican Foundation for Rural Development, and the Mexican Federation of Private Family Planning Associations (FEMAP) have used U.S funds to carry out their health care and development programs. By offering training, institutional and program support, research grants, and technical assistance in essential fields like community health, child survival, AIDS prevention, sanitation, and microenterprise development, these programs helped to maintain political stability while Mexican government social service cutbacks were pulling the rug out from under vulnerable populations.

United States aid could not have been more timely. On top of the crash of the early 1980s, Salinas' economic restructuring squeezed the middle and lower classes hard. Wage controls and price increases wiped out the purchasing power of Mexican workers and professionals alike, and labor unions were too weak and too tied to the government to guard against further erosion of their members' living standards. By signing on to the government's economic solidarity pacts, Mexico's major unions gave the go-ahead to Salinas' programs, even as their members suffered.

Government cutbacks, private sector bankruptcies, and slow growth meant too few jobs for the country's work force, which grows by nearly one million new job hunters each year. Unemployment climbed, standing in the early 1990s at about 18 percent. Those who do have work often scrimp together meager livings in the informal sector, pooling their earnings with other household members in order to get by. According to the United Nations' Economic Commission on Latin America, underemployment in Mexico, such as that found in the informal sector, afflicts 40 percent of the country's work force. Half the country lives in poverty, lacking adequate housing, health care, and basic services.

Washington's aid programs helped offset some of the effects of the crisis and the restructuring by providing a social safety net and helping create employment alternatives like microenterprises. Given the Mexican government's austerity budgets of the 1980s, many of these programs might never have started up and would almost surely have been eliminated had they relied exclusively on government sources of support. In the case of family-planning services, for example, AID pointed out in 1984 that "Mexico's economic crisis . . . sharply reduced the financial resources needed to maintain public support of social services, including family planning."[121] Lowering birth rates was already a major objective of the Mexican government, which hoped to get the annual population increase down to 1 percent by the year 2000. AID helped Mexico keep from losing ground in its effort to lower birth rates—with all the implications for food production, job creation, health care, education, housing, infrastructure development, and migration. In fact, as an AID strategy plan noted in 1990, "far and away" the largest share of the Washington office's contribution for programs in Mexico went to population programs: some $5.7 million in 1990.[122] Working through voluntary organizations and government institutions, AID not only guaranteed that programs would not be cut back but actually helped Mexico expand its population control services.[123]

Other programs, such as microenterprise development and support for community and national health care, also helped keep a safety net under some of the people at risk from Mexico's economic crisis and its new economic strategies. Organizations like ADMIC (Asesoría Dinámica a Microempresas) and the Murrieta Foundation used AID funds to offer credit, technical assistance, and training in a "free enterprise philosophy" to small businesses in both urban and rural areas. The Mexican Foundation for Rural Development, for example, helped establish apiculture enterprises in Chiapas and Oaxaca and provided training in honey production and business management.[124] AID has also provided training for rural health promoters, pharmacists, physicians, and nurses in maternal and child health care. Likewise, Ministry of Health personnel have been trained in child survival technologies like oral rehydration therapy.

Washington's aid programs do not concentrate solely on these safety-net operations. One of the newer initiatives will mean a big boost in conservation and environmental funding. Because Mexico was declared a "key" country in the effort to combat global warming, assistance to conservation projects intended to curb deforestation and air pollution climbed dramatically since 1990.[125] Other types of programs, such as training in wildfire suppression and search and rescue, media campaigns to prevent drug abuse, and scientific research grants have also received AID funding.

Even with the cutbacks, programs carried out with U.S. development aid tend to reinforce the asymmetry that already characterizes the relationship. According to AID, its projects are intended to "acquaint potential leaders [in Mexico] with [U.S.] societal and cultural values, develop trade and investment relations between the United States and [the Mexican] private sector, and increase the utilization of U.S. technology."[126] Developing such linkages is a key objective of AID assistance packages in Mexico—as in other advanced developing countries. The idea is to hook up U.S. institutions with Mexican counterparts so that U.S. expertise, goods, and services will flow steadily into the country. As AID explained

in 1984, "The proximity and diversity of U.S. technologies in almost all areas corresponding to Mexico's needs make the U.S. a
highly attractive source."[127] Using education, strategies, skills,
technology, equipment, and management techniques designed
mostly in the United States, these programs increase the dependence of Mexican recipients on U.S. counterparts.

Another problem is that these programs may not always meet
Mexico's long-term development needs. For example, Mexico
needs to develop backward linkages to multiply the economic
benefits of the maquiladoras. The country needs to foster its own
technological and agricultural base so that it will not always have
to base its development strategies on cheap labor. And microenterprises, while perhaps providing short-term economic relief to a
few worker-owners, may be seriously threatened by collapsing
trade barriers and potential competition from outside the country.

Food Aid

In tandem with Mexican government initiatives like the Solidarity program, U.S. food aid programs helped the Mexican government carry out economic transformations that might otherwise
have had to be scrapped because of political fallout. From 1983
through 1992, surplus U.S. food commodities helped compensate
for cutbacks in Mexican social programs, providing a safety net
for some of the sectors hardest hit by Mexico's restructuring. Over
the years commodities such as powdered milk, corn, cheese, rice,
wheat flour, and sorghum were distributed to needy populations
or sold on the market to raise funds for development activities.

Most of the food aid to Mexico went through the Section 416
program of the Commodity Credit Corporation.[128] The U.S. donations started up in 1983, coinciding with the worst years of Mexico's economic crisis. Programs like Section 416 recognized the
reality of Mexican poverty and the crucial role government welfare
and subsidy programs played in keeping the lid on discontent. As
a consequence, even though Mexico was identified as an advanced
developing country in other U.S. government programs, it was one
of the world's largest recipients of Section 416 donations.[129] In
1989 Mexico was second only to India as a recipient of Section
416 commodities.

Thanks to Section 416 donations, the Mexican government's social welfare agency, DIF, was able to expand its feeding programs, even while the government was cutting out ambitious consumer and producer subsidy programs like the Sistema Alimentaria Mexicana (SAM). But such efforts had more than just humanitarian objectives. They resulted in plenty of political currency for the PRI government, which used the food distribution and companion community development activities to extend its outreach and generate goodwill among many of those most immediately affected by the restructuring. But these programs were less helpful where the chronically poor were concerned, a fact pointed out by an AID assessment in 1990.[130]

Undergirded by U.S. food aid, the Mexican government had more political freedom to maneuver when carrying out its radical reforms of the country's economy. Without such support, pressures for more populist responses to the country's economic dilemma would likely have increased, perhaps to the boiling point in those parts of the country hardest hit by government cutbacks, privatization, agricultural restructuring, and other changes. Aside from offering a possible threat to the country's stability, such opposition might well have endangered the new policies themselves, outcomes thoroughly opposed by both the U.S. and Mexican governments.

Modernizing the Military

The warming of relations between Washington and Mexico City also strengthened the bonds between the U.S. and Mexican military establishments. Mexico's armed forces are still among the most nationalistic in the hemisphere, but the growing role of the Mexican military in antidrug operations and the government's emphasis on providing the armed forces with updated equipment and training opened the way to increased assistance from the United States.[131] By licensing commercial sales, providing training, leasing equipment, and supporting military sales to Mexico, Washington has backed the modernization of the Mexican armed forces and advanced the country's antidrug activities.

Military aid to Mexico reinforces long-term U.S. interests while helping to bolster the Mexican government's control over social sectors like labor and rural populations disrupted by the economic crisis and subsequent restructuring. Ensuring domestic order has been the military's main concern since the 1940s. Under Salinas, however, the military stepped up its police functions, intervening much more frequently when political and labor discontent flared into confrontation.[132] As far as it is possible to tell, Washington's aid to the Mexican armed forces has not been directed specifically at supporting these police functions. Instead it has helped strengthen the military institution by providing access to updated equipment and training, thus making the task of social control more easily accomplished. The Mexican government's wish to keep control over restive sectors of the population dovetails with Washington's interests in a "secure, stable, and friendly" southern neighbor.[133] Aside from guaranteeing a peaceable southern border, though, staying on friendly terms with Mexico and its military forces helps protect U.S. access to strategic raw materials, including petroleum, strontium, fluorspar, and antimony.[134]

But Washington wants more than stability on its southern flank. It wants Mexico to look to Washington for cues and technical support when it comes to international policies, whether military or otherwise. Security assistance to Mexico's military encourages just such a turn toward the United States, as do other U.S. aid programs.[135] As the Department of Defense told Congress, U.S. military programs in Mexico have the goal of "expanding U.S. influence in the [Mexican] military."[136]

Obtaining this influence in Mexico has not been easy compared with doing so in many other Latin American countries. In relative terms, military assistance to Mexico and the size of the U.S. military presence there have been very low, partly because Mexico's own military budget is small. In 1989, for example, Mexico's expenditures on its armed forces amounted to only about 0.6 percent of the GNP, one of the lowest in the hemisphere.[137] Although U.S. security aid to the country climbed during the late 1980s, almost all of it went to the Mexican Attorney General's office for antidrug programs.

Despite these caveats, the United States, more than any other country, has maintained a steady influence on the Mexican armed forces, one that is, however, tempered by Mexico's own independent and nationalist approach to the relationship. In one of the few close looks at the subject, Stephen J. Wager explained that "geographic proximity, a common border, and easy access to equipment and training material have contributed to the creation of a special relationship between both countries, a relationship which has by no means enabled U.S. influence to become dominating or pervasive."[138]

The broad outlines of this ambivalent relationship took shape during World War II and the early postwar years.[139] The threat of fascism first drew the two countries together, resulting in a Joint Mexico-U.S. Defense Commission. After the war, however, the commission became inactive and differences in their approaches to international politics pulled the two countries farther apart. Mexico refused to accede to such U.S. initiatives as the Rio Treaty, a hemisphere-wide mutual defense pact concluded in 1951 and designed to forge links among the U.S. and Latin American militaries. In contrast with the rest of the region, Mexico barely participated in U.S. security assistance programs. It received almost no support under the Military Assistance Program (MAP), a U.S. grant program that finances the purchase of defense articles and services, training, and technical assistance.[140] Likewise, the United States has not had a Military Assistance Advisory Group (MAAG) stationed on Mexican territory. Symbolically this fact—that a MAAG has not been deployed in Mexico—underscores the country's fierce independence from Washington when it comes to military ties; other than tiny Caribbean countries, Cuba is the only other Latin American country to share this distinction.

Most of the direct assistance that does occur is in the form of training. The International Military Education and Training Program (IMET) is key to increasing U.S. access to the Mexican armed forces. IMET is a cornerstone of U.S. military programs around the world, providing training for military personnel and their civilian colleagues either in the United States or at facilities abroad. Mexico sends more military personnel to the United States for training than to any other country.[141] Although in numerical terms the number of annual trainees is relatively small, the program is instrumental in building ties between armed forces in the two countries. As Elliott Abrams, assistant secretary of state for Latin American affairs under President Reagan, observed, Mexico is a country "where our access to the military results from and depends to a large degree on IMET."[142]

With the exception of funding for drug control activities, discussed in a later section, IMET has been the major source of direct U.S. military aid to Mexico during the postwar years. From 1946 to 1992 the United States provided almost $5.8 million for trainings under IMET.[143] Over the last few years the IMET grants have financed professional military education, maintenance courses, and instruction in how to operate and maintain antidrug equipment. IMET programs in Mexico increased sharply during the 1980s. During the three decades from 1950 to 1978, some 906 Mexicans participated in these training programs. From 1984 to 1992, however, some 575 Mexican military personnel were trained through IMET, with another 150 trainees scheduled in 1993.[144]

The modernization of the Mexican military that began in the early 1980s received important backing from commercial and government military sales supported by Washington. Although it does not receive U.S. funding for the purchases, Mexico buys U.S. equipment, spare parts, and technical assistance through the Foreign Military Sales Financing Program (FMS), a government program designed to support military sales to foreign countries. This has historically been a small program in Mexico, but it was stepped up in the 1980s. From 1946 to 1989 Mexico made more than $45 million in purchases through FMS, with two-thirds of the transactions occurring after 1987.[145] In fact, between 1982 and 1990, Mexico leased or purchased more military goods and services via the FMS system, commercial sales, or transfers of excess defense articles than it did in the previous three decades. Mexican leases or purchases of U.S. military goods and services totaled $29.5 million from 1950 to 1978. That figure skyrocketed to $500 million from 1982 to 1990.[146]

A top beneficiary of purchases and leases undertaken in the 1980s has been the Mexican Air Force, although the army has also benefited. Through programs like FMS Mexico purchased a squadron of F-5E aircraft, as well as Bell 212 helicopters, C-130 transport planes, and other aircraft.[147] The country leased U.S. UH-1H helicopters and purchased a variety of jeeps, light trucks, and other vehicles. Communications equipment, weapons, and spare parts also came through U.S. government channels.[148]

Fighting the Drug War

Most military-related assistance that has gone to Mexico in the past few years has been targeted for antidrug activities. After the

Salinas and Bush administrations took office in the late 1980s, the two countries began working closely on drug control programs, achieving a level of cooperation not seen since the 1970s. Because of Mexican sovereignty concerns and the fact that antidrug efforts are considered law-enforcement operations, it is difficult to get detailed information about current U.S.-Mexico drug control activities. Totals on the amount of U.S. funding or good descriptions of the types of activities on which the two countries work together are closely guarded by the responsible agencies. According to one DEA agent who asked to remain anonymous, some initiatives that would be public information if they occurred in other countries are classified with regard to Mexico because of that country's nationalist sensitivities.

Until 1993, Mexico traditionally received the largest amount of U.S. annual expenditures for foreign drug control. From 1978 to 1990 the Department of State's Bureau of International Narcotics Matters (INM) provided $150.3 million to Mexico as assistance for drug control activities, with more than half that amount provided after 1986.[149] In 1991, INM contributed nearly $20 million to Mexico, with a similar amount provided in 1992.[150] As with other U.S. government aid programs, however, direct aid to Mexico was cut back in 1993. The INM currently funds only U.S. activities related to the drug war in Mexico, and the Mexican government has picked up its own share of the tab.[151]

Until 1993, however, INM provided about a quarter of the Mexican Attorney General's annual budget for drug control, according to Elizabeth Carroll, Mexico desk officer at INM. Even with cutbacks in government-to-government aid, official U.S. assistance is likely to continue in the form of contracts with private firms. Such contracts are already in force in both eradication and high-tech communications activities and could be expected to climb with the drop in government-to-government aid.[152]

Besides INM, other U.S. government agencies have helped support Mexico's antidrug activities. One of these agencies is the Department of Defense (DOD). Much of DOD's support has been in the form of trainings through the International Military Education and Training program, which has averaged just under a half-million dollars a year since the mid-1980s. Some of these trainings teach Mexican personnel how to operate and maintain equipment used in antinarcotics activities.

DOD has also donated surplus equipment to Mexico for the drug war under presidential drawdown authority granted by the Foreign Assistance Act of 1961. In 1991, for example, DOD transferred twenty-one UH-1H Huey helicopters to Mexico, boosting the year's antinarcotics aid to $48 million.[153] And in early 1992, President Bush authorized the DOD to donate helicopters, spare parts, support equipment, and technical assistance valued at $26 million to the Mexican government.[154] Besides the defense contributions, agencies such as the Drug Enforcement Administration (DEA) and AID provide services that support antidrug work in Mexico but that are not included in the INM budget figures.

All aspects of the drug war, including detection, eradication, intelligence, and interdiction, have been supported by U.S. antidrug assistance. Over the years the aid has boosted the technological capabilities and professional skills of Mexican law-enforcement and military forces with training and equipment. INM, for example, has funded trainings, usually offered through U.S. law-enforcement agencies like the FBI, DEA, and the U.S. Customs Service, that focus on everything from sniffer dog training to techniques for combating money laundering. Likewise, Cessna Citation surveillance aircraft from the U.S. Customs Service track cocaine smugglers as they fly north from Colombia to landing strips in Mexico. The information is then relayed to Mexican law-enforcement agencies to help them interdict the traffickers. Law-enforcement agencies in each country work together on joint investigations, sharing information and evidence needed to disrupt trafficking networks.

Demand reduction is financed too, through the Agency for International Development and U.S. Information Service (USIS). AID, for example, spent nearly $2 million on demand-reduction programs in Mexico in 1991.[155] Working with Mexican private organizations, AID supported antidrug education and research programs. Some of these programs were aimed at youth—AID sponsored dance performances dramatizing problems relating to drug abuse, for instance. Likewise, one USIS project supported the creation of an antidrug music video and record album aimed at young people in Mexico.

Most of the direct aid from INM supported the aerial eradication program. The United States had provided some backing for these efforts since the 1970s, but during the Bush administration, the U.S. program expanded to include several components besides procurement and maintenance of aircraft. By the late 1980s INM was providing funds to purchase herbicides and fuel for the Mexican air fleet. For a time, it also paid salary supplements for Mexican pilots, mechanics, and other technicians, although that program was discontinued and the salary boosts are now paid by the Mexican government. During the early 1990s, INM support to the eradication program was primarily used for a maintenance contract with Bell Helicopter Services to keep the air fleet in good running condition.[156] Even so, Mexican drug-interdiction planes and helicopters have been plagued by mechanical problems, and in at least one case a helicopter crashed due to engine failure.

Mexico's Office of the Attorney General coordinates the drug control efforts in the country, and most U.S. aid has been funneled through that office. Under U.S. law, aid cannot be provided to police or law-enforcement officials in foreign countries in order to support or train them in programs involving internal intelligence or surveillance. But the DEA and the Federal Bureau of Investigation (FBI) are exempt from these restrictions if they are helping foreign law-enforcement officials fight the drug trade.[157] As an example, under the Administration of Justice program—a hemisphere-wide U.S. aid program aimed at police and judicial structures—the FBI taught forensic courses and basic law-enforcement skills to Mexican officers.[158]

Despite restrictions, Mexico's police forces have received support from agencies besides DEA and the FBI, including the U.S. military. The U.S. Army, for instance, provided technical assistance to the Mexican Office of the Attorney General.[159] And training sessions sponsored by the Customs Service and Coast Guard have helped law-enforcement and military forces learn investigative skills. Customs, for instance, conducted a course in financial-enforcement programs for investigators from the Mexican Treasury and Central Bank. According to a cable from the U.S. Embassy in Mexico City to the secretary of state, Customs also "supports [the antinarcotics] intelligence and training needs" of Mexico's Customs Service and the Federal Judicial Police, and has helped Mexican drug interdiction officers in the fields of "search, seizure, and evidence collection," under the Administration of Justice program.[160] Likewise, the Coast Guard has trained Mexican Navy personnel in interdiction and vessel-boarding procedures.

Another example is U.S. aid to Mexico's Northern Border Response Force (NBRF). Known as *Operación Halcón* in Mexico, the force was established in the late 1980s to enhance Mexico's aerial interdiction capability in northern border regions. Early interdiction efforts were successful, leading cocaine traffickers to set up new air routes and landing strips in different parts of the country. As a result, the NBRF now serves a nationwide area, although its effectiveness has diminished sharply at the same time.[161]

A rapid response team composed of agents from the Mexican Federal Judicial Police, the NBRF has received a large amount of high-tech support from the United States. Much of the equipment came from the United States, bringing a need for U.S. technical assistance at the same time. A U.S. Customs program, for instance, trained the team's pilots to use the sophisticated radar equipment and communications devices used in the program. Customs also taught Mexican team members how to fly and repair the U.S.-made aircraft used to track smugglers' planes as they come up from South America. Similarly, the U.S. Embassy in Mexico City set up a counternarcotics Tactical Analysis Team to relay U.S. Air Force intelligence to Mexican drug authorities about trafficking activities. The embassy team also helps Mexican officials coordinate operations and plan activities.

In addition to programs like these, the U.S. and Mexican governments are conducting negotiations and devising bilateral agreements to advance the drug war. A new Mutual Legal Assistance Treaty, for example, provides mechanisms for sharing evidence needed for prosecutions in each country. Another instrument, the Tax Information Exchange Agreement, provides means by which the two countries can exchange information on criminal and tax cases against traffickers and money launderers. Under the U.S.-Mexico Binational Commission, working groups meet periodically to discuss thorny issues like extradition and draw up frameworks for agreements. In a related vein, the two countries are working together to provide demand-reduction programs to Central American governmental and nongovernmental organizations. And, in recognition of Mexico's own expertise, the Organization of American States has used Mexican trainers and epidemiologists to carry out demand-reduction programs under its auspices.

Although less vigorous and dynamic than other aspects of the U.S-Mexico relationship, the growing ties between the militaries and police forces of the two countries are important. Training programs, for example, transmit U.S. national and regional security perspectives, along with technical skills and military tactics. Collegial relationships sparked by sharing problems and expertise during these classes can be expected to persist into the future. Just as important, the fact that Mexico is acquiring so much in the way of U.S. defense equipment and services means that the country will need to stay hooked into U.S. supply lines for spare parts and technical assistance.

Whatever the merits of wanting a strong Mexican security system to help guarantee stability and, as a consequence, U.S. interests, these military aid and antidrug programs inspire ethical concerns. As long as the Mexican armed forces continue to act as back-up police forces to quell disturbances that result from the government's authoritarianism and economic restructuring, U.S. military aid is helping to reinforce strong-arm approaches in the country.[162] Similarly, the Mexican military has been accused of human rights abuses while conducting antidrug operations.[163] Bolstering the repressive arm of the Mexican government may help to ensure that the country's radical economic reforms become fully entrenched and that drug production and trafficking are curtailed. Given the authoritarianism for which the Mexican government is known, however, the human costs of such programs may be too high to pay.

Democratization and the Perfect Dictatorship

From the day he took office, Salinas kept the throttle wide open as he steered the country toward an outward-looking market economy, while simultaneously dragging his feet on reforms to the country's authoritarian political system. By emphasizing economic over political reform—wagering that foreign investment, trade, and modernization would stimulate economic growth and good will toward the PRI—Salinas hoped to "keep the 'perfect dictatorship' from unraveling."[164] Some reforms did occur—opposition parties won a few governorships, for example, the first ever lost by the PRI—but for the most part Salinas explicitly put off political changes so that the government's centralized power could be used to guarantee that the economic changes would go through.[165]

Washington, which has promoted "democratization" as one of the major pillars of its recent foreign aid programs, looked the other way as political repression and electoral fraud continued under Salinas.[166] As shown by the U.S. assistance programs described above, the Reagan and Bush administrations actually bolstered the Mexican government, while not pressuring Mexico to liberalize politics as rapidly as the economy.[167] Whether this pattern will change under Clinton is still not certain. Some new U.S. government-funded programs have supported civic organizations aligned with the opposition, but as of yet there is little sign that Mexican democracy is as important in Washington as good trade and investment relations.

In general, Washington has always been more interested in Mexican stability than in its fortunes—ill or fair—in terms of democratic processes. Since the latter half of the nineteenth century, Washington has generally accepted whichever government was running the show in Mexico, as long as political stability was maintained. Indifferent to the dictatorial excesses of Porfirio Díaz in the years before the Mexican Revolution and mostly silent about human rights abuses and one-party dominance under the PRI, Washington has offered virtually no assistance for democratization efforts across its southern border.[168] To some extent this inaction has been justified as deference to Mexican sovereignty concerns. Looking at the big picture, though, suggests that Mexican sovereignty is just a smokescreen: Washington readily ignores such worries when its policy makers condition economic aid and debt management packages on Mexico carrying out economic-liberalization and austerity measures.

For a short period in the mid-1980s, Washington was somewhat more active on the democratic front, but even those efforts were primarily confined to rhetoric and admonitions. Moreover, the timing of Washington's interest in the fairness of Mexico's political system was significant. The years of greatest attention coincided with Mexico's economic crisis, the PRI's loss of standing among the electorate, the strengthening of conservative political parties like the National Action Party (PAN), and clashes with the Mexican government over U.S. policies in Central America. Loosening the governing party's grip on power during those years would likely have improved the electoral chances of conservative forces that shared the economic and political views of the Reagan administration. When in 1988 it appeared as if the demand in Mexico for political openings would favor the center-left opposition and not ideological allies in the PRI or the PAN, Washington openly threw its support to the PRI, ignoring the fraud-riddled election that brought Salinas into office.[169]

Some U.S. programs have purported to build democracy in Mexico, although until recently these have mostly aided the conservative opposition or traditional PRI forces. Since 1985, for instance, the National Endowment for Democracy (NED) has funneled U.S. government grants to a few Mexican organizations (see Table).[170] Until 1992, most of the grants supported Mexico's economic transformations, in keeping with NED's philosophy that a free market complements, and is a requirement for, political liberalization. In addition, most NED grants in Mexico were funneled through the most conservative of the endowment's core grantees: the Center for International Private Enterprise and the National Republican Institute for International Affairs (now known as the International Republican Institute).[171]

Nearly half of NED's grants to Mexico from 1985 to 1991 went to business organizations promoting free-market economies and advocating economic liberalization.[172] For instance, NED sponsored grants to train journalists in free-market economics and to help them place their economic policy op-ed pieces in Mexican newspapers. NED also funded the "Young Entrepreneur" training program of the Mexican affiliate of Junior Achievement, the Mexican Entrepreneurial Development Program (Desem). Desem later became a recipient of funding from the Agency for International Development. Other NED grants went to associations representing business interests, including Coparmex and Concanaco—Mexico's leading confederation of business organizations. From 1987 to 1988, for example, Coparmex received $173,118 to distribute a program teaching free-market principles in Mexico's technical-vocational schools. Likewise, Concanaco received a major grant to help its member chambers of commerce improve their skills in political advocacy. NED also financed training courses for Mexico's government-backed union and a conference for conservative Latin American political parties. The conference was co-sponsored by the PAN and coincided with the party's fiftieth anniversary.

Over the years, the major recipient of NED grants in Mexico has been the Democracy, Solidarity, and Social Peace Association

(Demos Paz) and its parent organization, the Superior Institute for Democratic Culture (ISCD). Grants to Demos Paz and the ISCD are channeled through NED's core grantee linked to the U.S. Republican Party, the International Republican Institute (IRI). Of all NED's grants in Mexico, those to Demos Paz have totaled the most in dollar terms and have spanned the greatest number of years. From 1988 to 1992, Demos Paz received $451,000 from NED. Another $120,000 grant was awarded in January 1993.[173]

An organization mostly composed of middle-class social christians, libertarians, and conservatives, Demos Paz is close to the PAN but not directly affiliated with the party. Demos Paz has only limited influence on the majority of Mexico's population, partly because of its middle-class focus. The organization sponsors seminars and produces publications, most of which are critical of the PRI and of the state of democracy in Mexico. These educational forums tend to have relatively few participants and are not aimed at developing a broad social movement. The organization also conducts monthly public opinion polls in Mexico City. These too, however, are targeted mostly at the middle class, with an average sample size of only 400 to 500 people. The relevance and reliability of these polls is limited by class factors, sample size, and the fact that the subjects are all from a single large urban area.

Looking at the above grants suggests that NED's role in Mexico has been conservative, and sometimes even irrelevant. In 1992, however, NED got directly into the electoral arena. The focus of the endowment's grants moved away from actively promoting free-market policies. With the PRI taking on such a pro-market mantle since Salinas took office, there is less need for NED to advocate such reforms. Instead NED's recent grants have concentrated more on politics per se than the endowment's earlier grants did.

The organizations receiving NED grants for their election-related activities since 1992 are the Council for Democracy (Consejo para la Democracia), the Convergence of Civic Organizations for Democracy (Convergencia de Organismos Civiles por la Democracia), and the Civic Front of San Luis Potosí (Frente Cívico Potosino).[174] The grants supported trainings for election monitors, "quick counts" during elections in Sinaloa and Chihuahua, publications, conferences, and some infrastructure development.

The Mexican grantees are known among democracy activists and Mexico watchers for their solid support for electoral democ-

T a b l e . *NED's Grant Allocations*

Organization Name	U.S. Pass-through Grantee*	Description of Organization	Purpose of Grants	Years	Funding Amount
Confederation of Mexican Workers	FTUI	Mexico's largest official trade union	Education programs and training seminars	1985	$100,000
Center for Studies in Economics and Education	CIPE	Nonprofit research institute in Monterrey	Seminars for Mexican journalists on economic policy and theory; support for production and distribution of op-ed pieces	1986	33,000
Coparmex	CIPE	Voluntary business organization representing 34,000 Mexican businesses	To continue its Empresa program, teaching free market economic principles in Mexican technical-vocational schools	1987-88	173,118
Democracy, Solidarity, and Social Peace Association (Demos Paz)	NRIIA/IRI	Nonprofit organization focusing on civic education and training	To conduct opinion polls, sponsor seminars and conferences, produce publications, and hold briefings for the press	1988-1992	451,000
NRIIA	NRIIA/IRI	International arm of the U.S. Republican Party	To convene a July 1989 conference of conservative Latin American political parties cosponsored by the PAN	1989	50,000
Mexican Entrepreneurial Development Program (Desem)	CIPE	Mexican counterpart to Junior Achievement Program	For its "University Impact" program, teaching private enterprise to students at University of Monterrey	1989	40,000

Organization Name	U.S. Pass-through Grantee*	Description of Organization	Purpose of Grants	Years	Funding Amount
Concanaco	CIPE	Mexico's leading confederation of business organizations	To improve individual chambers of commerce in their advocacy of the private sector	1990	111,506
Council for Democracy & Convergence of Civic Organizations for Democracy	NDI	Mexican civic organizations focusing on democratization issues	Technical and financial assistance to domestic civic groups observing elections in Sinaloa. Support for efforts at increasing electoral participation, including independent vote count in Chihuahua	1992	156,779
Council for Democracy	Resources for Action	Private organization for electoral reform in Mexico	To expand its program of election observation, "quick counts," publications, and forums	1992	60,000
Civic Front of San Luis Potosi	Resources for Action	Civic group in San Luis Potosi (supported Salvador Nava's campaign)	To support its new civic education school, offering courses on human rights, leadership skills, civic education, and increased women's participation in public affairs	1992	55,000

* CIPE–Center for International Private Enterprise. FTUI–Free Trade Union Institute. IRI–International Republican Institute. NDI–National Democratic Institute for International Affairs. NRIIA–National Republican Institute for International Affairs.

SOURCE: NED annual reports, 1985-1992, and board meeting minutes and grant documents.

racy and their opposition to the way politics are currently struc-
tured in the country. The Council for Democracy, for example, is
an association of prominent Mexicans whose permanent members
include journalists, academics, politicians, and political activists
from all three major parties. But these people mostly lend their
names to the association which is, in reality, a one-man show
headed by Julio Faesler. Faesler, a former member of the PRI, is
now linked to the PAN. He is known as a political moderate who
is trusted by U.S. organizations like NED and the National Democratic Institute for International Affairs. Although NED's 1992
grant was to help the council recruit new members, the organization still relies on activists mobilized by other groups to help carry
out tasks like vote counts and election observation.

The Convergence of Civic Organizations for Democracy (Convergencia) is more left of center than the council. Set up by activists in
nongovernmental organizations and popular organizations, Convergencia is closer to the PRD than to any other political party. It represents a coalition of some 136 groups representing twenty Mexican
states and the Federal District in Mexico City. Since 1991, Convergencia has organized election observations in seven states and in
Mexico City. NED, however, has not funded Convergencia's election
observations, instead supporting the group's seminars on election
monitoring and its trainings for poll watchers.

The Civic Front of San Luis Potosí is the most broad-based of
these three grantees. The Civic Front was a creation of Salvador
Nava—a leading member of the PAN who until his death was recognized as one of the most coalition-minded of Mexico's democracy activists. The group received $55,000 from NED in 1992 to
support a school for civic education and to improve its outreach
to other civic organizations and political sectors around the country. Nava also helped set up a powerful national network, the Citizens' Movement for Democracy (Movimiento Ciudadano
Democrático). Filled with firebrands, the Citizens' Movement for
Democracy includes the Civic Front as a regional affiliate and is
coalition-oriented in its approach to Mexican politics. Among its
members are activists in the PAN and PRD, reformist elements in
the PRI, and independent political activists. It has not been a recipient of NED grants, at least as of this writing.

Despite the broader range of support for groups from various
political tendencies, NED's grants still seem to be most favorable

toward either the PRI-dominated status quo or toward center-right parties like the PAN. This is most clearly seen by comparing funding levels. Election-related grants for individual organizations since 1992 have averaged around $68,000, with two grants going to Faesler's Council for Democracy, an organization that is closer to the PAN than to other political parties. The other major NED grants since that time have gone to Demos Paz, another center-right critic of the current Mexican government. But the funding picture is not completely black and white. Demos Paz, for example, is not opposed to working with left-of-center political organizations and parties. In fact, for a short time, the Citizen's Movement for Democracy had its national office at the ISCD.

The focus—at least to date—on poll watching and quick counts raises another doubt about the value of NED's grants in Mexico. These are obviously important tasks in Mexico, where fraudulent elections are the norm. But the effectiveness of these activities is limited both because of the size of the country—there are too many polling places to be covered—and because so much of the fraud and distortion of the political process takes place well before the elections. Biases in the federal electoral commission, for example, which is dominated by the PRI and tied to the Interior Ministry, make it virtually impossible for opposition parties to get fair treatment of their complaints. Human rights violations, irregularities during voter registration, manipulation of the voter lists, patronage programs, and the government's domination of Mexican media all contribute to a playing field tilted in the PRI's favor. If these issues remain unaddressed, quick counts and election monitors even risk the chance of validating election results because the voting itself was relatively free of overt fraud, while the combined irregularities over time would add up to an election climate that was unfair and invalid.

So far, NED's grants have not had the broad agenda suggested by this list of problems. The 1993 proposals to NED, however, reportedly have a wider focus, ranging from supporting pressure for changes in the structure of the electoral commission, to coalition building and message development among the opposition parties. NED has also been talking with another national citizens' group, the National Accord for Democracy, or ACUDE. ACUDE, like the Citizens' Movement for Democracy, is considered a potent, broad-based organization headed by politically sophisticated activists capable of mobilizing large masses of people. Whether NED will fund these activities or these organizations is not yet clear.

Besides NED, the other major conduit for U.S. government support to overseas political activities is the Agency for International Development. Even though AID has made promoting democracy one of the central pillars of its international activities, it has no such programs in Mexico. In fact, the agency's Mexico office stated in its 1991-92 Action Plan that democracy-building activities would be "counterproductive" in Mexico.[175] Ruling out projects in such areas as legislative procedures, election reform, or encouraging political pluralism, AID/Mexico—after consulting with the U.S. Embassy in Mexico City—instead urged increased support for its Administration of Justice (AOJ) programs in Mexico. A small, interagency AOJ program was run in Mexico for a couple of years in the early 1990s, but its focus was not democratization. Instead its projects supported trainings, conferences, and visitor exchanges aimed at Mexico's law-enforcement and legal communities, many of which overlapped with antidrug efforts.[176]

Mexico's progress toward democracy depends above all on its own internal processes, but the fact that the United States has chosen not to emphasize democratization as strongly as it has pushed economic liberalization undermines political reforms while shoring up authoritarianism. Making this observation is not a call for U.S. intervention in Mexico's political affairs. Washington's interference in Mexican politics would not resolve the country's democracy dilemma. Worse, as in countries like Nicaragua, such intervention would indeed violate Mexican sovereignty and is not advocated here.[177]

The new administration in Washington may indeed move questions regarding Mexico's treatment of human and political rights higher on its priority list, although as of mid-1993 the evidence on that possibility is mixed. Whatever the impact of U.S. political aid programs, democratization in Mexico is a crucial issue for the two neighbors. In many ways Mexico and the United States seem bound to a common future. The economic integration of the two countries makes such a common future probable, and partnership in NAFTA, should the accord be ratified, would assure it. With the politics and economies of the two countries increasingly intertwined, the state of democracy in each becomes a foreign policy as well as a domestic concern.

Chapter 3

Conclusion

The official programs of the U.S. and Mexican governments are only one component of a relationship that is getting broader and more complex every day. From nongovernmental organizations (NGOs) that promote human rights to cross-border networks focusing on the environment and public health, the two countries are being joined together by a web of actors in and out of government.

Even more important than the budding cross-border relationships of NGOs and activist groups are the momentous economic changes that are bringing the two countries together. Money and business are integrating North America. Economic forces—far more than transboundary migration, drug trafficking, or government programs—are pulling Mexico and the United States together. Between the United States and Mexico, as elsewhere in the world, big business has been the driving force in breaking down nationalist boundaries and promoting integration.

The evolution of national economies into integral elements of an emerging global economy is probably the most important factor in shaping the changes in U.S.-Mexican relations. The government leaders that have presided over these changes over the past decade or so—Reagan, Bush, and Clinton in the United States, and de la Madrid and Salinas in Mexico—responded to these new economic forces with open arms. They dismantled boundaries between the two countries that impeded trade and investment and stepped up government programs designed to encourage and support the cross-border activities of businesses and investors. At the same time, they enhanced joint efforts on shared problems like drug trafficking and environmental degradation, achieving by the early 1990s a level of cooperation and good will that has been rare in U.S.-Mexican relations.

But the increasing closeness of the two governments is not the whole story. North-South tensions continue to strain the relationship. For all its efforts, Mexico remains mired in the development problems of the third world, and the United States seems less intent on building bridges between North and South than on finding ways to bolster its economic hegemony. At the border, the fences only seem to get higher, the customs checks more thorough, and the social and economic divisions more severe. The line between the two countries seems not just an arbitrary barrier but one established by a timeless order that separates rich from poor, industrialized from underdeveloped, and the powerful from the weak.

Over the long term, the types of policies and programs instituted by the governments in Mexico and the United States will respond to domestic needs for stability and economic well-being that are complicated by these North-South differences. In the United States, for example, Clinton's policies will be determined in part by how successful he is in revitalizing the U.S. economy. Given the depths of the economic problems in the United States— from decayed infrastructure to a declining educational system— Clinton's chances of success are questionable. But if he cannot turn things around in the United States, it is likely that protectionist pressures from his constituents will grow stronger, threatening initiatives like NAFTA and government programs that aid Mexico. That trend is already evident in the cutbacks in U.S. development assistance to the country.

Mexican policies and programs will also be driven by economic needs, as well as by traditional North-South concerns such as sovereignty. Mexico is already facing such extreme pressures in the domestic economy that unemployment, poverty, and dislocation are feeding political movements that challenge the government's legitimacy as well as its credibility. With U.S. aid cutbacks, the extra source of stability for the Mexican government provided by programs like food aid and development assistance will be weakened. Given recent trends, the Mexican government will likely respond by opening the economy even more and pursuing trade relations with vigor—even if NAFTA gets defeated.

What these examples make clear is that if economic dynamics are driving the transformation of U.S.-Mexican relations, they do not stand alone. Government policies and programs create the framework and rules for integration. So far, these policies and programs have favored businesses and the stability of the Mexican government more than laying the foundation for an economic and political system with broadly distributed gains. Quieting critics with food aid and loans for microenterprises may have purchased the Mexican government time to entrench its new economic programs. But stopgap measures like these cannot advance equitable development over the long term. Achieving democracy and economic well-being will require a widespread distribution of economic and political power that government programs—whether U.S. or Mexican—have not yet treated with urgency.

References

1. Cathryn L. Thorup, "U.S. Policy-making toward Mexico: Prospects for Administrative Reform," in Rosario Green and Peter H. Smith, eds., *Foreign Policy in U.S.-Mexican Relations* (San Diego: Center for U.S.-Mexican Studies, 1989), 157.

2. During his tenure, Miguel Alemán steered government policies away from the extreme nationalism and populism of previous Mexican presidents. A probusiness conservative supported by financiers and industrialists, he encouraged tourism, commercial agriculture by large-scale private interests, big business, and market policies. He also brought the Mexican army under civilian control and limited its power, a remarkable achievement in Latin American politics. Alemán's policies found favor in Washington, and a warm relationship characterized the period.

3. Neoliberalism holds that reducing the size of the government and removing all barriers to free market activities will produce economic growth that will eventually benefit everyone.

4. Interview with Eric Fredell, 28 July 1993.

5. If ratified by the legislatures in Canada, the United States, and Mexico, NAFTA will join the three countries of North America in a free trade area designed to eliminate most trade barriers and stimulate foreign investment.

6. The labor accord, for example, allows sanctions only for violations of child labor laws, minimum wage guidelines, and health and safety protections. But violations of fundamental worker rights, such as freedom of association and the right to organize, could not result in trade sanctions under the accord. Exempting such protections means that labor suppression—a common problem in Mexico—could continue without recourse under NAFTA. The effect would be downward pressure on wages and working conditions in the United States as competition between U.S. workers and Mexican counterparts increased under the free trade agreement. Just as worrisome is the fact that omitting protections for worker rights from NAFTA represents a step backward for the United States, which includes provisions protecting internationally recognized worker rights in other preferential trade policies, such as the Generalized System of Preferences.

7. This careful study of the relations between the federal governments in each country does not mean that other relationships—state, local, and nongovernmental—are unimportant. As integration has advanced, linkages between U.S. and Mexican counterparts at these levels have proliferated at a dizzying rate. An extensive array of actors, including government agencies, environmental groups, health-care organizations, labor and human rights groups, and community activists have been developing ties with those sharing common interests and concerns on the opposite side of the border. With interests and objectives often competing with those of the national governments, this "citizen diplomacy" is helping to shape the bilateral agenda, especially around issues such as the environment. Two surveys of the expanding ties among U.S. and Mexican organizations are Ricardo Hernández and Edith Sánchez, *Cross-Border Links: A Direc-*

tory of Organizations in Canada, Mexico, and the United States (Albuquerque: Inter-Hemispheric Education Resource Center, 1992), and Gail Sevrens, *Environmental, Health, and Housing Needs and Nonprofit Groups in the U.S.-Mexico Border Area* (Arlington, VA: World Environment Center, June 1992). See also Cathryn Thorup, "The Politics of Free Trade and the Dynamics of Cross-Border Coalitions in U.S.-Mexican Relations," *Columbia Journal of World Business* (Summer 1991).

8. Quoted in Norman Gall, "Can Mexico Pull Through?" *Forbes*, 15 Aug. 1983, 79.

9. The U.S. Department of State promotes the view that U.S. and Mexican interests are converging. See, for example, the summaries of participant commentaries from its conference on "United States and Mexico: Converging Destinies" (Washington, DC: 4-5 April 1991). See also William D. Rogers, "Approaching Mexico," *Foreign Policy*, no. 72 (Fall 1988).

10. Bilateral Commission on the Future of United States-Mexican Relations, *The Challenge of Interdependence: Mexico and the United States* (Lanham, MD: University Press of America, 1989), 26.

11. GATT is the 105-member body formed after World War II to establish rules governing international trade and services.

12. This function as a doorway to Latin America reportedly prompted a large-scale U.S. intelligence presence in the country. The CIA sent its first agents to Mexico in 1948, only a year after the agency's creation. Press reports, former agents, and former U.S. government officials have indicated that, at least in earlier years, the CIA's station in Mexico was among the largest in the world. The CIA helped to establish a training school for Latin American unionists in Mexico, and it used the country as a post for keeping watch on Cuba. For example, the Mexican government allowed the CIA to monitor travelers to and from Cuba who came through the Mexico City airport. Until the early 1970s, Mexican authorities also permitted the CIA to tap the phones of Cuban diplomats both at the Cuban Embassy and in their Mexican homes. For more on the CIA in Mexico, see: Manuel Buendía, *La CIA en México*, 2nd ed. (Mexico: Aguilar, León y Cal Editores, 1990); Alan Riding, *Distant Neighbors: A Portrait of the Mexicans* (New York: Alfred A. Knopf, 1985), pp. 343, 344, 347, and 355; Philip Agee, *Inside the Company: CIA Diary* (New York: Stonehill Publishing Co., 1975), pp. 385 and 614; and Bob Woodward, *Veil: The Secret Wars of the CIA 1981-1987* (New York: Simon and Schuster, 1987).

13. Address by Carlos Salinas de Gortari to the Joint Session of the Congress of the United States of America, Washington, DC, 4 Oct. 1989.

14. The signs of what economists and political scientists call U.S. "decline" are multiplying at a frightening rate. Over the decade of the 1980s, the U.S. debt quadrupled. During the mid-1980s, the debt was climbing by a staggering $12 billion each month. When totaled, the U.S. foreign and domestic debt equaled about $4 trillion in the early 1990s—roughly ten times the foreign debt of all the countries of Latin America combined. The United States is now the world's largest debtor, and its borrowing over the decade left behind very little of lasting value, although Washington did help stimulate the world economy during the worst of the recession years by letting the dollar become considerably overvalued and running huge budget deficits that prompted U.S. demand for foreign goods. That "orgy of unfunded expenditure," as one historian described it, fueled speculative investments, a consumer spending spree, and a massive military buildup, but it resulted in little productive investment. Garry Wills, "Can Clinton Close the Vision Gap?" *New York Times*, 8 Nov. 1992, E17. See Sherle R. Schwenninger, "Reinvigorating the Global Economy," *World Policy Journal* (Summer 1992):432, for a discussion of U.S. debt-led growth during the early 1980s.

15. Robert A. Pastor, "The Latin American Option," *Foreign Policy*, no. 88 (Fall 1992).

16. For a concise and readable overview of these problems and their origins, see Schwenninger, "Reinvigorating the Global Economy," 429-48 (n. 14).

17. President Bush announced the Enterprise for the Americas Initiative (EAI) in late June 1990, just weeks after announcing the planned free trade talks with Mexico. The objective of the program is eventually to link all the countries in the Western Hemisphere in a free trade area governed by neoliberal economic principles. The hemispheric free trade area would be constructed gradually, working step by step through bilateral and multilateral trade agreements with eligible countries. In the meantime, the EAI offers access to the U.S. market, financial and technical resources, and some help with debt reduction to countries that liberalize their trade and investment policies, cut back government spending, and generally adhere to neoliberal economic prescriptions. For more on the EAI see: Betsy A. Cody and Raymond J. Ahearn, *The Enterprise for the Americas Initiative: Issues for Congress* (Washington, DC: Congressional Research Service, 30 Oct. 1992); Peter Hakim, "The Enterprise for the Americas Initiative: What Washington Wants," *Brookings Review*, Fall 1992; and "Enterprise for the Americas Initiative," interview with Xabier Gorostiaga, *Free or Fair Trade?* no. 1 (Bogotá, July 1992).

18. The need to expand exports in a protected regional market also brought Washington closer to Latin America as a whole, prompting programs like the Enterprise for the Americas Initiative and stimulating trade and investment. In 1991, for example, U.S. exports to Latin America (excluding Mexico) climbed by 20 percent, a rate nearly three times as fast as exports to the world as a whole and four times as fast as exports to the European Community. Latin America/Caribbean Business Development Center and the Agency for International Development, "U.S. Exports to Latin America Show Steady Gain," *LA/C Business Bulletin*, Nov. 1992.

19. Presidential Statement, White House, 12 Aug. 1992.

20. Comments made by Professor Jorge Castañeda, National Autonomous University of Mexico, on the draft of this chapter.

21. Cable from the U.S. Embassy, Mexico City, to all U.S. Consulates in Mexico, Cable No. 918868, 17 April 1991.

22. In contrast to this optimistic view, the Commission for the Study of International Migration and Cooperative Economic Development (Asencio Commission) found that an improved economic climate in Mexico would likely lead to increased migration, at least in the short term. The commission, which was established by the Immigration Reform and Control Act of 1986, said that the creation of low-paying jobs in Mexico would provide more people with the resources needed to head north for better-paying jobs. It predicted that even if Mexico's economy were to improve sharply as a result of a free trade agreement, it would take at least five years for wages and living standards to rise enough to slow migration to any substantive degree. Commission for the Study of International Migration and Cooperative Economic Development, *Unauthorized Migration: An Economic Development Response* (Washington, DC, 1990). Also see the research on NAFTA suggesting that migration will increase as a result of disruption in Mexico's agricultural sector: Sherman Robinson et al., *Agricultural Policies and Migration in a U.S.-Mexico Free Trade Area: A Computable General Equilibrium Analysis* (Berkeley: Department of Agricultural and Resource Economics, 1991).

23. Cable from the U.S. Embassy (see n. 21).

24. Those scars have not all healed. A few sectors of Mexican society—progressive academics and labor groups, for instance—still harbor fears and resentment of U.S. domination. Much of Mexican society, however, had already rejected intense anti-Americanism even before the late 1980s, as revealed by the quick acceptance of pro-U.S. policies and the new rhetoric of cooperation under Salinas. Many authors have written about U.S. intervention in Mexico and the wounds it left on the relationship. One of the most sensitive treatments by a U.S. observer is found in the chapter on U.S.-Mexico relations in Riding, *Distant Neighbors* (see n. 12).

25. Sally Cowal, speaking at the U.S. Department of State conference on "United States and Mexico: Converging Destinies" (see n. 9).

26. The meeting took place in Mexico City. López Portillo was quoted in Riding, *Distant Neighbors*, 321 (see n. 12).

27. Quoted in ibid.

28. For a review of Carter's approach to Mexico, and its contrast with policy making under Ronald Reagan, see Thorup, "U.S. Policy-making toward Mexico" (n. 1).

29. Ibid., 150.

30. More information on Mexican foreign policy and its effects on bilateral relations is found in: Tom Barry, ed., *Mexico: A Country Guide* (Albuquerque: Inter-Hemispheric Education Resource Center, 1992), 71-74; Riding, *Distant Neighbors*, 340-363 (see n. 12); and Green and Smith, *Foreign Policy in U.S.-Mexican Relations* (see n. 1).

31. Washington's first Mexican bailout occurred in 1976 under Republican President Gerald Ford. The 1982 intervention was much more extensive, however, involving the advance purchase of Mexican oil for the U.S. Strategic Petroleum Reserve, support from the U.S. Treasury and Federal Reserve Bank, rescheduling payments to commercial banks, import credits for grains and basic foods, and a standby agreement with the International Monetary Fund that required Mexico to impose severe austerity measures. See James H. Street, "Mexico's Development Crisis," *Current History* 86, no. 518 (March 1987), and Sidney Weintraub, *A Marriage of Convenience: Relations between Mexico and the United States* (Oxford: Oxford University Press, 1990).

32. From a commentary by John Saxe-Fernandez in *Excélsior*, cited in *Latin America News Update*, Nov. 1990.

33. Quoted in Riding, *Distant Neighbors*, 323 (see n. 12).

34. Ibid., 360, and Bruce Michael Bagley, "Interdependence and U.S. Policy toward Mexico in the 1980s," in Riordan Roett, ed., *Mexico and the United States: Managing the Relationship* (Boulder, CO: Westview Press, 1988), 225-26.

35. Negroponte's "confidential" cable was directed to Bernard Aronson, assistant secretary of state for inter-American affairs. It was cited by *Proceso* (Mexico City), 13 and 20 May 1991.

36. One of the major signs of increased cooperation between the two countries was the creation of the U.S.-Mexico Binational Commission (BNC). This cabinet-level commission pulls together all the threads of the U.S.-Mexico relationship. Established in 1981 by presidents Ronald Reagan and José López Portillo, the BNC predated by several years the genial collaboration kicked off under Bush and Salinas, weathering some of the stormiest years in recent U.S.-Mexico relations. Buffeted by the many disagreements of the mid-1980s, the commission lost effectiveness and was nearly scrapped. But as testimony to the U.S. government's interest in Mexican oil, its concerns about Mexico's stability, Mexico's wish to climb out of its economic crisis, and shared interests in stimulating economic ties, Bush and Salinas reinvigorated the BNC. Composed of U.S. Cabinet members and their Mexican counterparts, the BNC is co-chaired by the U.S. secretary of state and the Mexican Foreign Secretary. The commission itself holds annual meetings but its working groups meet throughout the year to discuss topics of concern and devise joint responses. Among the U.S. agencies that have participated in BNC work groups are the Department of the Treasury, Department of Justice (including the FBI), Immigration and Naturalization Service, Environmental Protection Agency, Drug Enforcement Administration, and U.S. Information Agency.

37. Quoted in "Trade Zone Prototype?" *National Journal*, 29 July 1989, 1924.

38. Statement before the Subcommittee on Western Hemisphere and Peace Corps Affairs of the Committee on Foreign Relations, *Fiscal Year 1992 Foreign Assistance Request for the Western Hemisphere*, 102nd Cong., 1st sess., 18 and 25 April 1991, 10.

39. Dependency theory held that the underdeveloped South could not hope to catch up to the industrialized North through trade or investment. Once linked economically, development in southern countries would depend on and be secondary to the consumer needs and investment patterns of the North. On the one hand, the value of advanced products from industrialized countries would constantly increase relative to the value of goods from less developed countries. Trade between the two sets of countries would therefore always disadvantage the South. On the other hand, foreign investment would lead only to capital outflow through profit repatriation and foreign control over technology and management decisions. Moreover, the South's own development patterns would be shaped by the needs of the North—growing bananas, for example—because the North wanted them, or constructing processing plants, transportation networks, and communications lines to serve exporters and foreign investors, but not to fulfill local development needs. An outstanding survey of dependency theory and an application of one version to Mexico is Gary Gereffi and Peter Evans, "Transnational Corporations, Dependent Development, and State Policy in the Semiperiphery: A Comparison of Brazil and Mexico," *Latin American Research Review* 16, no. 3 (1981). For a review of dependency theory in the light of evidence that third world governments can promote development while integrated into the global economy, see Peter Evans, "After Dependency: Recent Studies of Class, State, and Industrialization," *Latin American Research Review* 20, no. 2 (1985).

40. There were many important factors besides fear of Mexican competition for U.S. markets that influenced Latin American governments to liberalize their economies. These included conditions attached to loans and other assistance from the United States and the international lending institutions, stagnant growth rates, a stubborn global slowdown, the failures of previous development strategies, and the discrediting of the Marxist alternative.

41. Cable from the U.S. Embassy (see n. 21).

42. Jill Abramson, "U.S.-Mexico Trade Pact Is Pitting Vast Armies of Capitol Hill Lobbyists against Each Other," *Wall Street Journal,* 25 April 1991, A16.

43. The U.S. Council of the Mexico-U.S. Business Committee is a committee of the Council of the Americas and is sponsored by the American Chamber of Commerce of Mexico and the U.S. Chamber of Commerce. Its counterpart in Mexico is the Mexican Business Council for International Affairs (CEMAI).

44. U.S. Council of the Mexico-U.S. Business Committee, "Statement of Purpose: Strategies for 1990-92," n.d.

45. Established to compensate for the fast-track provision written into the 1974 Trade Act, ACTPN is a major voice in trade negotiations and is the only statutory mechanism for including private sector input in trade negotiations. The Mexican Business Council on Foreign Trade (COECE) served as the private sector advisory committee on NAFTA for the Mexican government.

46. The 1987 Framework Understanding on Trade and Investment, for example, established a consultative mechanism to help resolve trade and investment issues, and to negotiate the removal of trade barriers. It acted as a vehicle for hashing out disagreements over trade and investment, providing for annual cabinet-level consultations but permitting more frequent meetings by policy specialists when necessary. In a more ambitious move, the Understanding Regarding Trade and Investment Facilitation Talks of 1989 mandated both a comprehensive negotiation process and joint study groups aimed at resolving disputes and devising agreements on specific issues.

47. John Watling, "State Trade Offices Pave Way for U.S. Businesses," *El Financiero International,* 15 June 1992.

48. Ann M. Veneman, U.S. deputy secretary of agriculture, in a news release on NAFTA, 13 Aug. 1992, and interview with Wendell Dennis, Foreign Agricultural Service, 4 Nov. 1992.

49. Interview with Dennis (ibid.).

50. Interview with Wendell Dennis, 12 Aug. 1993.

51. Under NAFTA, according to U.S. Deputy Secretary of Agriculture Ann Veneman, the United States expects export gains in meats (including beef, pork, and sausage), grains (such as corn, wheat, and sorghum), poultry, and horticultural products (including fresh apples, pears, peaches, fresh vegetables, and tree nuts). Veneman, news release (see n. 48). Products like these are already being exported in increasing quantities to Mexican markets.

52. According to Wendell Dennis of the Foreign Agricultural Service, "Europeans are putting out a greater and greater supply [of agricultural products] that is subsidized." There is a "considerable gap" between the U.S. domestic price and the world market price of certain commodities, Dennis said, explaining that the EEP helps compensate for that differential to keep U.S. businesses competitive. Interview with Dennis (see n. 48).

53. Foreign Agricultural Service, "Export Enhancement Program" (Washington, DC, June 1992).

54. Congressional studies in 1990 and 1991 found that U.S. government subsidies, credit guarantees, loans, set-asides, infrastructure support, research, marketing services, and other assistance provided a staggering 61.5 percent of the value of U.S. wheat producers' income in 1987. *Agricultural Trade: Government Support Calculations under the U.S.-Canada Free Trade Agreement* (Washington, DC: General Accounting Office, Aug. 1990) and *Agricultural Trade: Determining Government Support under the U.S.-Canada Free Trade Agreement* (Washington, DC: General Accounting Office, Feb. 1991).

55. "Grain and Feed Annual Narrative" (Mexico City: U.S. Agricultural Affairs Office, 1990).

56. Interview with Kathy Anderson, Foreign Agricultural Service, 1 Dec. 1992, and interview with Dennis (see n. 50).

57. Interview with Max Bowser, Foreign Agricultural Service, 13 Nov. 1990, and interview with Wendell Dennis, Foreign Agricultural Service, 1 Dec. 1992.

58. Interview with Susan Reed, Foreign Agricultural Service, 2 Dec. 1992.

59. Interview with Kevin Bernhardt, U.S. Department of Agriculture, 13 Aug. 1991.

60. "Annual Plan of Work" (Mexico City: U.S. Agricultural Affairs Office, 10 March 1988).

61. Among the participants in USDA market development programs in Mexico are the American Embryo Transfer Association, American Quarter Horse Association, Kentucky Distillers Association, National Dry Bean Council, Pillsbury Company, U.S. Mink Export Development Council, and USA Poultry and Egg Export Association. Information provided by the Foreign Agricultural Service, Nov. 1992.

62. One of the trade associations whose members benefit from U.S.-backed market development programs is the U.S. Feed Grains Council (USFGC). Among other projects, the USFGC sponsors demonstration farms in Mexico that work with major Mexican dairy farmers to enhance technology and skills, and to encourage them to buy U.S. feed and other supplies. The USFGC has been teaching Mexico's dairy producers to raise Holstein bull calves as a sideline to their dairy operations. Normally slaughtered within their first three days of life, the calves are being promoted by the USFGC as stock for the Mexican and U.S. beef industries. At the same time, the organization is encouraging the farmers to use U.S. feed grains for the calves. Ricardo Celma, "Mexico Ranks among World's Most Promising Markets for U.S. Feed Grains," *AgExporter*, March 1991, 11.

63. The U.S. Food Festival, held in July 1991, was the first food show in Mexico to focus solely on U.S. foods and beverages. It was co-sponsored by the Western United States Agricultural Trade Association, the Mid-America International Agri-Trade Council, the Southern United States Trade Association, and the FAS. Reflecting the surge of inter-

est in consumer-ready and high-value products, the show included exporters of frozen yogurt, pizzas, microwaveable foods, and frozen foods, as well as meat, wines, snacks, and other products. Interview with Bobby Richey, Jr., U.S. agricultural attaché, Mexico City, 4 March 1992, and Elizabeth Offutt, "New Trade Festival in Mexico to Spotlight U.S. Food and Beverages," *AgExporter*, March 1991.

64. Figures obtained from Wendell Dennis, Foreign Agricultural Service, Nov. 1992.

65. Interview with Dennis (see n. 48).

66. *U.S.-Mexico Trade: Trends and Impediments in Agricultural Trade* (Washington, DC: General Accounting Office, 1990), 34. Conasupo was the principal buyer of corn under GSM-102 as recently as 1991. Interview with Pat Haslach, Commodity Credit Corporation, 13 Aug. 1991.

67. The GSM-103 program, with repayment terms ranging from three to ten years, underwrites transactions on products with longer economic lifespans, like breeding livestock. Mexico was allocated $10 million in GSM-103 credit guarantees in fiscal year 1992, and it has been allocated $20 million in these credit guarantees for 1993. Interview with Amy Brooksbank, U.S. Department of Agriculture GSM program, 4 Nov. 1992.

68. Interviews with Brooksbank, ibid. and 2 Aug. 1993.

69. Interview with Brooksbank, 2 Aug. 1993 (see n. 67).

70. Interview with Richey (see n. 63), and Bobby G. Richey and Lynn Reich, "Credit Guarantee Programs Help Open Doors in Mexican Marketplace," *AgExporter*, March 1991.

71. Interview with Richey (see n. 63).

72. Although minimal in dollar terms, the Trade and Development Program's funding for infrastructure development in Mexico is aimed at "helping U.S. firms get in on the ground floor of projects that offer significant export opportunities" in the long run. It has supported hydroelectric, environmental, mining, and transportation projects in Mexico by providing funding for U.S. firms that carry out feasibility studies, consultancies, and other planning services. *Business America*, 4 Dec. 1989, and U.S. Trade and Development Program, *Congressional Presentation Fiscal Year 1992* (Washington, DC: Government Printing Office, 22 Feb. 1991).

73. Japan, for example, provided $805 million of untied credits for equipment and infrastructure to make lead-free gasoline and sulfur-free fuel and diesel oil, as well as to rehabilitate locomotives. Andrea Curaca Malito, "Japanese Assistance in Pollution Control Opens Door for U.S. Business," *Business America*, 8 Oct. 1990.

74. American Chamber of Commerce in Mexico, "The Role of Development Banks in U.S.-Mexico Trade," *Review of Trade and Industry*, 2nd q., 1992. By 1993, Mexico's percentage of Eximbank's total portfolio had dropped to about 17 percent. Based on figures obtained in interview with Don Schuab, Eximbank, 3 Aug. 1993.

75. Eximbank classifies countries according to the terms of an agreement worked out among member states of the Organization for Economic Cooperation and Development. In terms of income level, Mexico is considered an "intermediate" country. This allows interest rates below those of "rich" countries but above those of "poor" countries.

76. *Export-Import Bank of the United States: An Independent Government Agency that Assists the Financing of U.S. Exports*, pamphlet (Washington, DC: U.S. Export-Import Bank, Nov. 1990).

77. When loan guarantees and insurance were included, the total for those years exceeded $15.5 billion. *1987 Annual Report* (Washington, DC: U.S. Export-Import Bank); interview with Quang Phung, Eximbank, 26 Aug. 1991; and "Eximbank in Mexico," *Business America*, 4 Dec. 1989, 17.

78. Despite the large value of the portfolio devoted to Mexico, Eximbank's loans and credits held by Mexican buyers represented only about 10 percent of U.S.-Mexican trade

in 1991. John Watling, "Fast Finance: Where Big Banks Fear To Tread," *El Financiero International*, 23 Nov. 1992.

79. Interview with Schuab (see n. 74).

80. "Eximbank in Mexico," *Business America* (see n. 77).

81. Ironically, Mexican cement industries that have been benefited at least in part by Eximbank programs face tariff barriers when they export to the United States because they have been accused of selling their cement below cost. See "Penalties on Cement Exports to Continue," *El Financiero International*, 28 Dec. 1992.

82. The first loan guarantee to Pemex occurred in 1990, igniting a firestorm of criticism in Mexico. The bank guaranteed a $1.5 billion loan to Pemex for offshore exploration projects in the Bay of Campeche. As with other Eximbank programs, the conditions attached to the loan guarantee required Mexico to use U.S. firms to conduct the oil exploration and development projects that were planned. Mexican critics feared that the agreement would provide a back door into the Mexican oil industry, which was protected by provisions in the Mexican Constitution. Vindicating the critics, that first loan guarantee did foretell increased U.S. participation in the Mexican oil industry. Although the sector was kept off the table during NAFTA negotiations and foreign investors still may not own Mexican oil reserves, the government's deregulation of many petrochemicals and decentralization of Pemex opened the way for U.S. involvement in petrochemicals, exploration, plant building, and other types of investment. See, for example, Edward Cody, "Oil Loan Touches a Mexican Nerve," *Washington Post*, 7 Dec. 1990, and Thomas S. Heather, "Private Sector Participation in Petroleum," *Business Mexico*, Aug. 1992.

83. Mexico's sales to the Strategic Petroleum Reserve were discontinued in the late 1980s. From the late 1970s to 1988, Pemex sales to the Strategic Petroleum Reserve totaled 236 million barrels. Interview with John Bartholomew, Strategic Petroleum Reserve, 13 April 1993.

84. Watling, "Fast Finance" (see n. 78), and interview with Schuab (see n. 74).

85. The dividing line between explicitly promoting runaways and providing services that may inadvertently encourage such a move is a fine one. Recent press reports about AID programs in Central America, for example, show that AID helped fund training programs and advertising campaigns aimed at attracting U.S. companies to El Salvador and Honduras. See Doyle McManus, "U.S. Aid Agency Helps to Move Jobs Overseas," *Los Angeles Times*, 28 Sept. 1992, A1, and *Paying to Lose Our Jobs* (New York: National Labor Committee Education Fund in Support of Worker and Human Rights in Central America, Sept. 1992).

86. For a discussion of the legislation and arguments on both sides, see hearings before the House of Representatives Subcommittee on Commerce, Transportation, and Tourism of the Committee on Energy and Commerce, *Department of Commerce's Program to Promote Relocation of U.S. Industry*, 99th Cong., 2nd sess., 10 Dec. 1986. Also see Michael Moore, "Made in Mexico: Reagan Administration Encourages U.S. Businesses to Move Jobs South of the Border," *Multinational Monitor*, Feb. 1987.

87. Responding to criticism of these programs, one AID official angrily justified the initiatives: "Don't we want these economies to develop? Or do we just want to send sacks of grain, the way we do to Somalia, to keep people alive for another day?" McManus, "U.S. Aid Agency Helps to Move Jobs Overseas" (see n. 85).

88. Interview with Art Danart, Agency for International Development, 28 Oct. 1992.

89. University of the Americas, "Analisis de la rotación de personal en las industrias maquiladoras en Mexico" (proposal submitted to AID), July 1990.

90. Agency for International Development, *Action Plan for Fiscal Years 1985 and 1986* (Mexico City, Oct. 1984), 24.

91. Ibid., 27.

92. Agency for International Development, *Mexico: Action Plan, FY1991-92* (Washington, DC, April 1990), 15.

93. Ibid.

94. The following discussion on NAFTA is taken from an interview with Gerard Bowers, 4 March 1992.

95. *El Financiero International*, 25 Nov. 1992.

96. *Agence France-Press*, 20 July 1992.

97. Quoted in "Commission Nurtures Export Culture," *El Financiero International*, 30 Nov. 1992.

98. In Dec. 1990, for example, Charles Roh of the U.S. Trade Representative's office spoke with Juárez business leaders to promote the proposed free trade agreement. Cable from the U.S. Consulate in Juárez to the U.S. Embassy in Mexico City, Cable No. 901963, 12 Dec. 1990.

99. "Pending Foreign Principals," cumulative list of registered foreign agents for Mexico in the United States (Washington, DC: U.S. Department of Justice, 20 Nov. 1992).

100. For a rough layout of these trends, see ibid. See also: Jill Abramson, "U.S.-Mexico Trade Pact"; Peter H. Stone, "In Mexico, Lobbyists Strike Gold," *National Journal*, 19 Sept. 1992; Diana Solis, "Mexico Hires Numerous U.S. Lobbyists to Push Passage of Free Trade Accord," *Wall Street Journal*, 24 Sept. 1992; Herminio Rebollo and Leticia Rodríguez, "Mexico Spent 56 Million Dollars to Promote NAFTA in the U.S.," *El Financiero International*, 19 April 1993; and Tim Golden, "Mexico Tries to Bolster Political Image in U.S.," *Miami Herald*, 3 Jan. 1992.

101. Rebollo and Rodríguez, "Mexico Spent 56 Million Dollars" (ibid.). According to this report, which cites the government's public accounts documents, Mexico spent approximately $56 million during the 1990-92 period in consulting fees, operating expenses, salaries, media coverage, promotion, and public relations related to the NAFTA negotiations.

102. Brock was retained by Mexico through two separate contracts, one with the Brock Group, of which he is senior partner, and one with Burson-Marsteller, a leviathan in the public relations business. For his services with Burson-Marsteller, Brock received $30,000 a month. To handle public relations for Mexico, Burson-Marsteller was paid $323,000 per month, out of which it took cuts for subcontractors like Brock and the lobbying firm of Gold and Liebengood. Stone, "In Mexico" (see n. 100), and "Pending Foreign Principals" (see n. 99).

103. Stone, "In Mexico" (see n. 100).

104. Abramson, "U.S.-Mexico Trade Pact" (see n. 42).

105. For a detailed history of these relations, see essays by Jorge A. Bustamante, J. Angel Gutiérrez, and Rodolfo O. de la Garza in Tatcho Mindiola and Max Martínez, eds., *Chicano-Mexicano Relations* (Houston: University of Houston Mexican-American Studies Program, 1986).

106. Rodolfo O. de la Garza, "Chicanos and U.S. Foreign Policy: The Future of Chicano-Mexican Relations," *The Western Political Quarterly* 33, no. 4 (Dec. 1980):571-82.

107. Bustamante concluded at the time that the idea of the Mexican government looking to Chicanos as a lobby had been "discarded from the panorama of objectives." Jorge Bustamante, "Relación cultural con los Chicanos," *Uno Más Uno*, 11 Oct. 1982. Also see his "Chicano-Mexicano Relations: From Practice to Theory," in Mindiola and Martínez, *Chicano-Mexicano Relations*, 8-19 (n. 105). However, the creation in 1987 of the Program for Enhanced Relations between the Mexican government and the U.S. Mexican-American community did indicate continuing interest by the Mexican government in cultivating ties with Mexican Americans. Rodolfo O. de la Garza and Claudio Vargas, "The Mexican-Origin Population of the United States as a Political Force in the Borderlands: From Paisanos to Pochos to Potential Political Allies," in Lawrence A.

Herzog, ed., *Changing Boundaries in the Americas: New Perspectives on the U.S.-Mexican, Central American, and South American Borders* (San Diego: Center for U.S.-Mexican Studies, 1992), 89-111.

108. For more information see Secretaría de Relaciones Exteriores and Comunidades Mexicanas en el Exterior, *Programa para las comunidades Mexicanas en el exterior: Objetivos, políticas, campos de acción* (Sept. 1990).

109. Interview with Rodolfo O. de la Garza, University of Texas at Austin, 14 April 1993.

110. Southwest Voter Research Institute, *Latino Consensus on NAFTA* (San Antonio: Sept. 1993).

111. Cable from the U.S. Consulate in Hermosillo to the U.S. secretary of state, Cable No. 901640, 18 Dec. 1990.

112. This section deals with U.S. development aid, narrowly defined. Much more important to Mexico in dollar terms have been the enormous funds from multilateral lending institutions such as the World Bank and the International Monetary Fund. The seal of approval and financial support from these institutions constitute an indirect form of U.S. government assistance because of the major influence the United States wields in these forums.

113. Agency for International Development, *Mexico: Action Plan, FY1991-92*, 53-54 (see n. 92). Considering overall cutbacks in U.S. aid, along with increasing claims on aid funds from Eastern Europe and the fact that for several years Mexico has exceeded the cutoff level for aid in terms of per capita income, the level of funding through 1992 was significant. The information that Mexico had exceeded aid cutoff levels was obtained during an interview with Danart (see n. 88).

114. Interview with Babette Prevot, AID/Mexico desk officer, 29 July 1993.

115. More telling, most of AID's assistance to Mexico came in the form of loans Mexico was expected to repay. Riding, *Distant Neighbors*, 344 (see n. 12), and Agency for International Development, *U.S. Economic Assistance Programs Administered by the Agency for International Development and Predecessor Agencies* (Washington, DC, 1971), 35.

116. Riding, *Distant Neighbors* (see n. 12); Agency for International Development, *Action Plan for Fiscal Years 1985 and 1986*, 3 (see n. 90); and interview with Gerard Bowers, AID/Mexico, 26 July 1990.

117. Agency for International Development, *Action Plan for Fiscal Years 1985 and 1986* (see n. 90).

118. Interview with Bowers (see n. 116).

119. The expanding U.S. aid programs in Mexico (and in other "strategic" areas, such as El Salvador) were particularly ironic given the social service cutbacks being leveled against the U.S. poor during these same years of the Reagan administration.

120. Interview with Samuel Taylor, AID/Mexico, May 1989.

121. Agency for International Development, *Action Plan for Fiscal Years 1985 and 1986*, 7 (see n. 90).

122. Assistance in previous years was even higher, averaging $7.5 million in 1988 and 1989. Agency for International Development, *Mexico: Action Plan, FY1991-92*, 5 (see n. 92).

123. AID provided contraceptives—forty million condoms in 1986, for example—surgical supplies, training, equipment, and institutional support. It also promoted "voluntary surgical contraception," such as tubal ligation and vasectomies, and funded media campaigns to popularize birth control among Mexico's public.

Strong criticisms have been raised against population control programs like these that are promoted by developed countries in poorer countries like Mexico. Critics argue that the problems of global and national poverty are caused by an inequitable distribution of resources, not by overpopulation or scarcity per se. They also point out the classist and racist character of many of these programs, as they most often are directed against the poor and the nonwhite. The fact that the Reagan and Bush administrations provided funding for media campaigns around contraception in Mexico while remaining lukewarm to similar programs in the United States—even in the face of the AIDS epidemic—gives strong weight to these criticisms. See Eduardo Galeano, *Open Veins of Latin America: Five Centuries of the Pillage of a Continent* (New York: Monthly Review Press, 1973), for a passionate exploration of the relationship between poverty and inequitable distribution of resources in the Americas.

124. Agency for International Development, *Mexico: Project Assistance (Projects Active as of March 1991)* (Washington, DC, May 1991), 26. See also Agency for International Development, *Action Plan for Fiscal Years 1985 and 1986* (n. 90); Agency for International Development, *Mexico: Action Plan, FY1991-92* (n. 92); and Catherine Mansell Carstens, "Financing Mexican Microenterprise (Part II)," *Business Mexico*, Nov. 1992.

125. Agency for International Development, *Mexico: Action Plan, FY1991-92*, pp. 3, 20-22, 35, and 51-53 (see n. 92).

126. Agency for International Development, *Congressional Presentation Fiscal Year 1989* (Washington, DC, 1990), 283.

127. Agency for International Development, *Action Plan for Fiscal Years 1985 and 1986*, 4 (see n. 90).

128. Until 1972, Mexico received modest levels of support under three U.S. PL480 food assistance programs. With the exception of some PL480 Title II (food donations) commodities provided to the United Nations World Food Program for refugees in Mexico, the country no longer receives any PL480 assistance. For a closer look at PL480 programs in Mexico, see Barry, *Mexico: A Country Guide*, 379-80, n. 36 (n. 30).

129. From 1983 to 1991, Mexico received more than $300 million in Section 416 aid. Foreign Agricultural Service, "U.S.G. Section 416(b) Assistance to Mexico," 26 Aug. 1991, and Agency for International Development, *Mexico: Action Plan: FY1991-92* (see n. 92).

130. David L. Franklin, "Assessment of Section 416 Food Assistance Program to Mexico Summary Report," report prepared for AID/Mexico (Research Triangle Park, NC: Sigma One Corporation, Sept. 1990), 8.

131. On the changing role of the Mexican military, including its participation in civic action programs and its increasing involvement in subduing labor and civil disturbances, see David Ronfeldt, ed., *The Modern Mexican Military: A Reassessment* (San Diego: Center for U.S.-Mexican Studies, 1984). For a more recent overview of the Mexican military, see Roderic A. Camp, *Generals in the Palacio: The Military in Modern Mexico* (London: Oxford University Press, 1992).

132. See, for example, "Use of Troops a Cause of Concern in Mexico: Armed Forces Are Sent to Deal with Politics, Labor, and Crime," *New York Times*, 5 Nov. 1989.

133. *Congressional Presentation for Security Assistance Programs*, fiscal year 1992 (Washington, DC: U.S. Department of Defense, 1991), 217.

134. Mexico is the United States' second most important source of strategic raw materials. *Department of State Bulletin*, Oct. 1989.

135. In contrast to other U.S. aid programs, however, U.S. military assistance has been less successful in accomplishing a turn toward the United States. The Mexican military remains extremely nationalistic, with a fairly strong undercurrent of anti-U.S. sentiment.

136. *Congressional Presentation for Security Assistance Programs*, fiscal year 1989 (Washington, DC: U.S. Department of Defense, 1988), 248.

137. From 1950 to 1978, there were only a few countries in the region that received less military aid from the United States than Mexico did. These included various Caribbean microstates and several small countries such as Costa Rica, Haiti, and El Salvador.

Lars Schoultz, *Human Rights and United States Policy toward Latin America* (Princeton: Princeton University Press, 1981), 215, and Agency for International Development, *U.S. Overseas Loans and Grants and Assistance from International Organizations*, Obligations and Loan Authorizations, July 1, 1945-September 30, 1981 (Washington, DC, 1981). On Mexico's military spending, see *World Military Expenditures* (Washington, DC: U.S. Arms Control and Disarmament Agency, 1989).

138. Stephen J. Wager, "Basic Characteristics of the Modern Mexican Military," in Ronfeldt, *The Modern Mexican Military*, 100 (see n. 131).

139. This discussion of historical ties between the two militaries draws heavily on Wager's study in ibid. But for a brief overview of the notion of a U.S.-Mexico "security community," see also Paul Ganster and Alan Sweedler, "The United States-Mexican Border Region: Security and Interdependence," in David Lorey, ed., *United States-Mexico Border Statistics since 1900* (Los Angeles: UCLA Latin American Center Publications, 1990).

140. During the postwar period Mexico received less than $50,000 in support through the MAP. Agency for International Development, *U.S. Overseas Loans and Grants and Assistance from International Organizations* (see n. 137).

141. Wager, "Basic Characteristics," 101 (see n. 138).

142. Quoted in a commentary by John Saxe-Fernandez, *Excélsior*, 2 April 1991. Relationships with Latin American militaries forged during such U.S. programs have long been cultivated by the Department of Defense. As Robert McNamara, former secretary of defense, once explained to Congress: "I need not dwell upon the value of having in positions of leadership men who have the firsthand knowledge of how Americans do things and how they think. It is beyond price to make friends of such men." Statement before the House of Representatives Subcommittee on Foreign Operations Appropriations, Committee on Appropriations, *Foreign Operations Appropriations for 1963*, 1962, E59.

143. Agency for International Development, *U.S. Overseas Loans and Grants and Assistance from International Organizations* (see n. 137), and interview with Karen Garvey, Department of Defense, 28 July 1993.

144. These figures are drawn from several sources: Schoultz, *Human Rights* (see n. 137); Carmen Lira, "Desde 1982, México ha comprado a EU más armas que en los 30 años anteriores," *La Jornada*, 30 June 1989; interview with Maj. Michael González, Department of Defense, Latin America and Africa Division, 13 Sept. 1991; and interview with Garvey (ibid.).

145. Agency for International Development, *U.S. Overseas Loans and Grants and Assistance from International Organizations*, 56 (see n. 137); *Congressional Presentation for Security Assistance Programs* (Washington, DC: U.S. Department of Defense, 1983-1992); and hearings before a House of Representatives Subcommittee of the Committee on Appropriations, *Foreign Operations, Export Financing, and Related Programs Appropriations for 1991*, 426.

146. Lira, "Desde 1982" (see n. 144), and *Congressional Presentation for Security Assistance Programs* (ibid.).

147. *Congressional Presentation for Security Assistance Programs* (Washington, DC: U.S. Department of Defense, 1989), 248-50.

148. *Congressional Presentation for Security Assistance Programs* (Washington, DC: U.S. Department of Defense, 1992), 217.

149. Agency for International Development, *U.S. Overseas Loans and Grants and Assistance from International Organizations*, various years (see n. 137).

150. Interviews with Elizabeth Carroll, U.S. Department of State, Bureau of International Narcotics Matters, 3 Sept. 1992 and 29 July 1993.

151. Interview with Elizabeth Carroll, 29 July 1993 (ibid.).

152. Interview with Fred Schellenberg, CIA analyst at the El Paso Intelligence Center, 29 July 1992.

153. Tim Golden, "Mexico Says It Won't Accept Drug Aid from U.S.," *New York Times*, 26 July 1992.

154. "Memorandum of Justification for Presidential Determination Regarding the Drawdown of Defense Articles and Services for Mexico" (Washington, DC: U.S. Department of State, 8 Nov. 1991) and Presidential Determination No. 92-17, "Drawdown from Department of Defense Stocks for Counternarcotics Assistance for Mexico," 26 Feb. 1992.

155. Agency for International Development, *Mexico: Project Assistance* (see n. 124).

156. Interview with Carroll (see n. 150).

157. Robert L. Wilhelm, "The Transnational Relations of United States Law Enforcement Agencies with Mexico," *Proceedings of the Pacific Coast Council on Latin American Studies* 14, no. 2 (1987):161.

158. Cable from the U.S. Embassy, Mexico, D.F., to the U.S. secretary of state, No. 250128, 23 Oct. 1989.

159. Cable from the U.S. secretary of defense to Army Headquarters in Washington, DC, No. 221825Z, Jan. 1991, and cable from the U.S. secretary of defense to Army Headquarters in Washington, DC, No. 141130Z, Oct. 1990.

160. Cable from the U.S. Embassy (see n. 158).

161. *Drug Control: Revised Drug Interdiction Approach Is Needed in Mexico* (Washington, DC: General Accounting Office, May 1993).

162. In commenting on this section, Col. Stephen Wager, a historian and student of the Mexican military at West Point, said that the Mexican army grew more uncomfortable with performing police duties during the 1980s. Wager noted that senior officers complained to Mexican political leaders who then attempted to curtail such functions. Wager described Salinas' use of the army to control dissenting groups as a "deviation" from the general policy during the 1980s. Wager's observations are important, but the fact that the Mexican government uses the army as a reserve police force holds negative implications for human rights nonetheless.

163. See, for example, Americas Watch, *Human Rights in Mexico: A Policy of Impunity* (New York, 1990).

164. During a forum in Mexico City in 1990, Peruvian novelist Mario Vargas Llosa described Mexico as a "perfect dictatorship . . . camouflaged so that it appears not to be a dictatorship." An assessment of Salinas' emphasis on economic restructuring over democratization is undertaken in Douglas W. Payne, "Mexico: The Politics of Free Trade," *Freedom Review*, July-Aug. 1991, 26.

165. In mid-1993 the Mexican government proposed a number of electoral reforms that were being considered in the Chamber of Deputies. The proposals ranged from setting limits on campaign financing to eliminating the "governability clause" that guarantees majority control of the Congress to any party that wins 35 percent of the popular vote. The proposed reforms did not include changes to the federal electoral commission to make it more impartial, a critical omission in terms of Mexican democratization. See Ted Bardacke, "All the Right Moves," *El Financiero International*, 12 July 1993, 13.

166. For statements about the proclaimed importance of democratization in U.S. hemispheric policies under President Bush, see the testimonies of Bernard Aronson, assistant secretary of state for inter-American affairs, and James H. Michel, assistant administrator for AID's Bureau for Latin America and the Caribbean, before the Senate Subcommittee on Western Hemisphere and Peace Corps Affairs of the Committee on Foreign Relations, *Fiscal Year 1992 Foreign Assistance Request for the Western Hemisphere*, 102nd Cong., 1st sess., 18 and 25 April 1991. For detailed information about repression under the Salinas government, see: Amnesty International, *Mexico: Torture with Impunity* (London, 1991); Americas Watch, *Human Rights in Mexico* (n. 163); Americas Watch, *Unceasing Abuses: Human Rights in Mexico One Year After the Introduction of Reform* (New York, 1991); and Alicia Ely-Yamin, "Justice Corrupted,

Justice Denied: Unmasking the Untouchables of the Mexican Federal Judicial Police," paper prepared for the Mexico Project of the World Policy Institute (New York: New School for Social Research, 20 Nov. 1992).

167. One blatant example of Washington's support for the PRI and Salinas even in the face of government-sanctioned electoral fraud in Mexico occurred after the Nov. 1990 summit between Bush and Salinas. Just one week before the summit, the PRI declared that its candidates had won all thirty-four legislative districts in the state of Mexico, where opposition candidate Cuauhtémoc Cárdenas had beaten Salinas two to one in 1988. Ignoring media analysts, opposition leaders, and other critics who cried fraud, Bush announced a $1.5 billion loan to the Mexican government to be backed by Eximbank.

168. For a close look at the specific question of U.S. support for democratization in Mexico, see Lorenzo Meyer, "Mexico: The Exception and the Rule," in Abraham F. Lowenthal, ed., *Exporting Democracy: The United States and Latin America* (Baltimore: Johns Hopkins University Press, 1991).

169. In a major show of support, President Reagan telegraphed congratulations to Salinas even before the election results were in. He then provided the new Mexican government with a $3.5 billion bridge loan.

170. Established in 1983, the National Endowment for Democracy (NED) is a privately incorporated grant-making institution funded by Congress. Active around the world, NED supports foreign political parties, trade unions, business groups, civic organizations, the media, and other important political sectors. For more on this institution, see Beth Sims, *National Endowment for Democracy: A Foreign Policy Branch Gone Awry* (Albuquerque: Inter-Hemispheric Education Resource Center, 1990).

171. NED has four "core" grantees, through which the bulk of its grants are funneled to foreign organizations. These are the Center for International Private Enterprise, Free Trade Union Institute, International Republican Institute, and National Democratic Institute for International Affairs. These are the international arms of the U.S. Chamber of Commerce, AFL-CIO, Republican Party, and Democratic Party, respectively.

172. Most of this information is drawn from the annual reports, board meeting minutes, and other documents of the National Endowment for Democracy, but also see Sims, *National Endowment For Democracy* (n. 170), and Barry, *Mexico: A Country Guide*, 326-27 (n. 30).

173. National Endowment for Democracy annual reports, 1988-1992, and National Endowment for Democracy board meeting minutes, 22 Jan. 1993.

174. The following discussion is taken largely from National Endowment for Democracy board meeting minutes, 1992-93, and grant proposals and grant reports from NED recipients.

175. Agency for International Development, *Mexico: Action Plan, FY1991-92*, 8 (see n. 92).

176. Interview with Arthur Danart, AID, 17 Nov. 1992; cable from the U.S. Embassy, Mexico City, to the U.S. secretary of state, Attachment D, 25 Oct. 1989; and information memorandum from Maria Mamlouk to AID's assistant administrator for the Bureau of Latin America and the Caribbean, 8 March 1991.

177. In Mexico, for instance, there has been nothing comparable to Washington's noisy denunciations of the Nicaraguan government under the Sandinistas, its subsequent insistence that elections there be declared free and fair by international observers, and its massive election-related aid to the opposition. For the best overview of Washington's aid to the main opposition coalition in Nicaragua's 1990 elections, see William I. Robinson, *A Faustian Bargain: U.S. Intervention in the Nicaraguan Elections and American Foreign Policy in the Post-Cold War Era* (Boulder, CO: Westview Press, 1992).

About the Authors

Beth Sims, a research associate at the Inter-Hemispheric Education Resource Center, is the author, co-author, or contributor to several books, including *The Great Divide: The Challenge of U.S.-Mexico Relations in the 1990s* (Grove Press, forthcoming), *Runaway America: U.S. Jobs and Factories on the Move* (Resource Center Press, 1993), *Workers of the World Undermined: American Labor's Role in U.S. Foreign Policy* (South End Press, 1992), and *Mexico: A Country Guide* (Resource Center, 1992). She received her Master's in Political Science from the University of New Mexico.

Tom Barry has been a senior analyst at the Inter-Hemispheric Education Resource Center since its founding in 1979. He is a co-author of *The Great Divide: The Challenge of U.S.-Mexico Relations in the 1990s* and is the author or co-author of all the books in the Resource Center's *Country Guide* series. He is the author of *Central America Inside Out* (Grove Weidenfeld, 1991), co-author of *Feeding the Crisis* (University of Nebraska Press, 1991), and author of *Roots of Rebellion* (South End Press, 1986).

Resource Center Press

Resource Center Press is the imprint of the Inter-Hemispheric Education Resource Center, a private, non-profit, research and policy institute located in Albuquerque, New Mexico. Founded in 1979, the Resource Center produces books, policy reports, audiovisuals, and other educational materials about U.S. foreign policy, as well as sponsoring popular education projects. For more information and a catalog of publications, please write to the Resource Center, Box 4506, Albuquerque, New Mexico 87196.

Board of Directors

Forthcoming from Grove Press, April 1994

The Great Divide

The Challenge of U.S.-Mexico Relations in the 1990s

Tom Barry, Harry Browne, and Beth Sims

▄▄"All international borders are at once fascinating and disconcerting . . . But it is not the contrasting cultures . . . that [make] crossing the U.S.-Mexico line so shocking . . . it is the experience of passing so rapidly between economic worlds."▀▀ — *excerpt*

The Great Divide is an in-depth examination of the U.S.-Mexico relationship—one that has often been volatile, characterized by prejudice, imperialism, and violence, and only recently by cooperation and mutual dependence. This precarious harmony is threatened by the potentially problematic ramifications of the North American Free Trade Agreement, which, if passed, promises to change permanently the nature of the relationship.

Bound as the U.S. and Mexico are by trade, debt, immigration, and the drug war, the economic and social issues that face both countries play out most visibly along the border. Nine thousand people a day cross illegally into the U.S. through the borderlands; 2,000 maquiladora factories spread across the border employ nearly 500,000 Mexicans and yet are subject to virtually no labor or environmental laws; 50 percent of the cocaine and 75 percent of the marijuana smuggled into the U.S. comes across the border; and the pollution in the area is so bad that a section of the Nogales Wash, a borderlands river, recently exploded.

This is another book in the Grove Press series which includes *The Central America Fact Book* and *Central America Inside Out*.

The U.S.-Mexico Series

The Challenge of Cross-Border Environmentalism:
The U.S.-Mexico Case

Few predicted the clout environmentalists now have in international trade discussions. Suddenly, environmental issues have become central to the rapidly evolving relationship between the United States and Mexico. *The Challenge of Cross-Border Environmentalism* explores diverse environmental issues—including cross-border air and water contamination, pesticides, pollution-haven investment, maquiladora wastes, sharing of water resources, and impacts of liberalized trade—and examines how governments and citizen groups are responding to new environmental challenges. The book, copublished by the Resource Center Press and the Border Ecology Project, focuses on conditions in the U.S.-Mexico borderlands where many of these problems and challenges are most apparent.

No. 1 in the series. ISBN: 0-911213-45-7. 121 pages, paperback, $9.95

Crossing the Line:
Immigrants, Economic Integration, and Drug Enforcement on the
U.S.-Mexico Border

Crossing the Line takes a close and current look at the U.S.-Mexico borderlands. It is along a common border that many of the challenges that face the two nations are most acutely felt. The society and economy of the borderlands reflect historic tensions and divisions between the two nations. At the same time, the increasing interdependence of the neighboring countries is most apparent in the border region. The book looks closely at the cross-border problems presented by the northward migration stream, the maquila economy, the booming narcotics trade, and the infrastructure crisis—problems that extend beyond the borderlands to the heart of U.S.-Mexico relations.

No. 3 in the series. ISBN: 0-911213-46-5. 146 pages, paperback, $9.95

For Richer, For Poorer: Shaping U.S.-Mexican Integration

Money and business are integrating North America. More than any other factor, they have brought the United States and Mexico closer together than at any time since the 1917 Mexican Revolution. The two countries' histories as leaders of the industrialized North and the developing South, respectively, make the emerging partnership a highly influential model for the rest of the world. Important sectors in both nations stand to benefit from closer integration, but the neoliberal economic policies that have cleared the way for booming cross-border trade and investment are wreaking havoc on workers, small businesses, and communities across the continent, and forcing people on both sides of the Rio Grande to come to grips with globalization for the first time. *For Richer, For Poorer* explains the nuts and bolts of globalization, the pros and cons of the free trade debate, and alternative strategies to promote a more balanced process of integration that advances workers' rights and the environment as well as business interests.

No. 4 in the series. ISBN: 0-911213-47-3. 100 pages, paperback, $9.95

**Include $3.00 shipping and handling for the first book,
50¢ for each additional. Prices subject to change.**

**Resource Center
Box 4506 / Albuquerque, NM 87196
(505) 842-8288**